COPING
W H E N

A Parent

Dies

COPING W H E N

A Parent

Dies

Janet Grosshandler-Smith

THE ROSEN PUBLISHING GROUP, INC./NEW YORK

Published in 1995 by The Rosen Publishing Group, Inc.
29 East 21st Street, New York, NY 10010

First Edition

Library of Congress Cataloging-in-Publication Data
Grosshandler, Janet.
    Coping when a parent dies / Janet Grosshandler-Smith.—1st ed.
       p.   cm.—(Coping with series)
    Includes bibliographical references and index.
    ISBN 0-8239-1514-X
    1. Grief in adolescence.   2. Grief in adolescence—Case studies.
3. Bereavement in adolescence.   4. Bereavement in
adolescence—Case studies.   5. Parents—Death—Psychological
aspects.   6. Teenagers and death. [1. Death. 2. Grief.]
I. Title. II. Series: Coping with series (New York, N.Y.)
BF724.3.G73G77   1995
155.9'37—dc20   94-23320
                                         CIP
                                         AC

Manufactured in the United States of America

Contents

ABOUT THE AUTHOR ◇

Janet Grosshandler-Smith is a guidance counselor at Jackson Memorial High School in Jackson, New Jersey. Helping teenagers work through difficult problems in their lives has always been a priority in her life.

Janet earned her BA at Trenton State College in New Jersey and soon followed with an MEd from Trenton while teaching seventh grade English. Working as a guidance counselor for the past sixteen years has given her a wide range of experiences with adolescents. Making a difference in people's lives by loving them and helping them is Janet's focus.

Janet's first husband died in 1989 after a battle with cancer. She was left to raise her young children on her own. Experiencing and processing grief has been her own journey.

Janet lives in Jackson with her second husband, Rudy Smith, and their sons, Nate, Jeff, Mike, and Rudy. She squeezes in time for running and reading.

CHAPTER 1

Tara's Story

Your teenage years are filled with so many changes: happiness, turmoil, achievements, sadness, love, friendship, depression, romance, incredible highs, and some very low experiences.

But what about death? How does a teenager cope with death? What happens to you if your parent passes away? What are these jumbled-up feelings and how do you sort them out?

Most of the time, there is power in youth itself. On the football field, you can fight hard to win. In school, you can strive to get good grades. You can communicate and work out problems at home. You've been told that if you put effort, brain power, and muscle into a problem, you can solve it. You can have a second chance.

That is not the case with death.

"There are enough crazy things going on for teens," said Tara, a senior in high school. "But when my mother died four years ago, everything in my life changed. It was as if I skipped from the age of fourteen to eighteen so fast. I had to take on more responsibility at home and grow up quickly. I had to deal with a lot of things that most teens don't even have to think about."

Feeling alone, scared, angry, relieved, shocked, numb, depressed—all these emotions and more are normal reactions for a teenager when a parent dies. You feel a terrible aching sadness for a long, long time.

"I kept expecting Mom to be there," Tara said. "I would set the table for all of us, and then it would hit me all over again—*WHAM!* She's not here. She won't be sitting with us at this table ever again. It hurts so much."

Losing your mother or father, whether it is after a long, lingering illness such as AIDS or cancer, or in a shockingly quick manner, such as in a car accident or by gunshot, may make you feel that your world has come to an end. How can you accept that your mother or father, whom you loved, has really died?

Dr. Elisabeth Kübler-Ross has written a number of books about death and dying. She is recognized as an expert in understanding grief. Grief is the process by which you react and respond to the losses in your life. Grief is an emotion that can affect your physical health, your ability to think and focus on a task, and your relationships with other people.

Going through the grieving process is useful and healing. In order to work through your grief, you have to deal with the feelings, thoughts, and decisions that the death of a loved one brings about.

Dr. Kübler-Ross has placed into categories all the crazy, mixed-up feelings you experience when your parent has died. The stages of grief usually include shock, denial, anger, bargaining, depression, and finally realization and acceptance. There is no set order in which these reactions occur.

"When my mother was in the hospital for those last weeks, getting thinner and thinner, sicker and sicker," said Tara, "I felt like I was on a seesaw. I wanted her to live because I loved her so much, but I also hated to see all her pain and how the cancer was just destroying her body and her spirit.

"I blocked a lot of it out. Sometimes I just pretended that she would get better, come home, and life would go back to normal. I wanted that so badly. I used to pray to God that if he cured my Mom, I'd go to church all the time and never fight with my parents anymore—all weird stuff just hoping that God would answer my prayers."

Tara was "bargaining," hoping to hold off the frightening thought that her mother might not get better and could die. She wanted God to answer her prayers. It is said that God does answer prayers, but sometimes the answer is "No."

"Mom came home from the hospital when there wasn't any more they could do for her. She was on real strong medicine, but she knew where she was and that we were all with her. My Dad, my brother, sister, and I were all there holding her hand when she died. It may sound scary to want to be with someone when they die, but I wanted to be with my mother. She knew I was there and it helped me face her death.

"Everyone is there for you at the wake and the funeral. But you're kind of numb, in shock, then. After everyone goes home, the small shocks set in. Dinners change, the routine of the house is different. Mom no longer comes home from work at the expected time. Coming into the house when it's so quiet and expecting to hear her say, 'Tara, is that you?' . . . I blocked out a lot of it. It was too painful."

Denial, which blocks out the pain and sadness, is not necessarily bad for people. It helps people function during a deeply disturbing time.

Functioning as if you are in a dream may keep you from crumbling into a deep depression. Denial gives you the time to readjust your thoughts. The reaction is certainly a normal one. You desperately want to believe that this is all a bad dream, a nightmare from which you'll wake up.

"People would say to me, 'I know how you feel,' and then I would get angry because I felt they couldn't really understand what I was going through," Tara recalled. "I had to let my anger out somehow. It wasn't fair. My mom was a good person. Why her? Why did *she* have to die? Why did this happen to me?"

Anger is a normal reaction. It may come from rage at the unfairness of your parent's death, or from hopelessness, or even guilt if you weren't getting along with your parent when he or she died.

You are frustrated at death. You don't understand it or want it in your life. You didn't choose for your mother or father to die. You feel helpless, and you may even feel angry at the parent who is still alive. Understand that you need to let these feelings flow through you. You are experiencing normal reactions to your loss.

Resentment is also a common feeling. When a parent dies, the routine of the family is thrown into upheaval.

"My sister and I had to take on the responsibility of the house," Tara said. "It was tough getting used to it. Mom had taken care of the whole house and now the two of us had a hard time getting it all together.

"Sometimes I felt it was unfair. My friends would invite me to go out and do something, and I had to do the food shopping or the laundry instead. I had to give up some of the fun things in order to do the household chores. My friends didn't always understand either. They'd tell me to leave it undone or let my dad do it. I couldn't. I just couldn't."

Depression is another emotion you will experience. You're dragging around not caring about anything. You just want to stay in bed and hide under the covers for a month. Everything is in turmoil and you're confused. You may resent other people who can smile or laugh. "How can they act so normal when my grief feels so terrible?" you ask yourself. You feel depressed, low, and nothing seems to work or go right.

Don't be afraid to cry. It is good to shed tears and allow the pain to work through your system. Express your grief, don't suppress it. You'll feel better afterward. You may find tears in your eyes at unexpected moments. This is all normal. All teenagers, boys and girls, should allow themselves to show their emotions. This will help relieve some of the depression.

"Holidays are the worst," Tara said. "Christmas, birthdays, the anniversary of Mom's death are all so hard to get through. Even now, four years later, there are days when I break down, but I have to get through them.

"Before, there were days when I felt like giving up. Then I'd think about Mom and ask myself, 'Is this what she'd want from me?' I'm lucky that I have a pretty strong self-image and self-discipline. I kept myself going, kept pushing myself to keep up my grades in school and do well. But it was hard, so hard some days."

After working through depression, Dr. Kübler-Ross holds that the final stage is acceptance. When you reach this stage, you are able to acknowledge the fact of death. There is no time limit on reaching this stage. Some people start accepting their loss in a few months. For others it may take years. You begin to be more at ease with yourself when you realize that nothing else can be done. Your mother or father has died, and no amount of denial, anger, bargaining, or depression can change that.

Reaching the acceptance stage may take a considerable amount of time and effort, but once you reach it, your healing begins.

Each person has his or her own way of expressing grief and working through the pain. You might need to take long walks alone or be with a lot of company. You might want to be very quiet or play loud music. Your sister may keep looking through the family photo albums, and you may not want to see them for months. You may need to explain what you are going through to your friends, so they can understand better how to help you.

During the early months of grief, you'll need to pay special attention to your own needs and those of other members of your family. There is no "right" or "wrong" way to feel. Find out what's best to help you work through things.

Get the help you need from other family members, friends, teachers, counselors, or professional people who are willing to aid you in coping with the death of your parent.

Understand that a mixed combination of emotions will flow over and through you, and whatever feelings you experience are normal reactions to losing your mother or father.

No longer a child, not quite an adult, teenagers have unique needs when experiencing grief. Seek help and let your feelings out so your healing can begin. Your sad feelings will never go away completely—there is bound to be a permanent scar—but the wound does heal.

As Tara said four years after her mother passed away,

"You don't ever forget, but it does get a little easier every day."

Like Tara, many young people will have parents die from illness or accidents. The shock sends people reeling no matter how it happens.

Lauren's father committed suicide, and her younger brother was the one who found him. How can she cope with this? What can any person do to put his or her life back on track in these circumstances?

With more and more guns being used everywhere, more people are being shot to death. In some places it's a daily occurrence. How can people deal with these overwhelming circumstances?

AIDS is more prevalent now and many teenagers may lose a parent to this disease. Whom can these teens talk to? How will this affect their lives? Where can they turn?

A parent may die from a drug overdose or alcoholism. What does a person say to people who know what happened? How can they get on with their lives?

Death and grief come into people's lives in very different ways. No two experiences are the same. This book explores the aspects of dealing with grief and describes how some teens have worked through the most difficult times of their lives. No one has to go through this alone. There are many things that can be done to help people cope with loss, and there are many people who are there to help.

CHAPTER 2

What Is Grief?

During your lifetime you will experience many kinds of loss. This is natural. This is normal. As a person changes and grows older, certain things in life are left behind. Feelings of loss are part of the growth process.

For example, if you ever have to move to a new town, leaving your old friends and familiar places, you may, in the beginning, feel sad and alone. Or when you move on to junior high school, leaving your old elementary school friends behind, you may have similar feelings. These losses fade away as the momentum of your new experiences takes over.

The feelings of loss caused by the death of a loved one are much more painful, traumatic, and overwhelming. This loss may or may not have been expected, and you will experience the sense of loss for a long period of time.

The grief you feel is normal and will actually have a healing effect.

Grief is the total process of reacting and responding to the great losses in our lives. Grief usually affects all aspects of your life. You will feel grief emotionally, in your heart, and you will feel grief psychologically, in your mind. Grief affects how you feel physically, and it also affects your relationships with other people.

Grieving is a *process*. It serves as a useful healing function when it is allowed to come out. The outcome of the grieving process should be the resolution, or coming to terms with the hurt you feel, and reestablishing your life. Grief allows you to work through all the feelings, thoughts, and decisions that this great loss brings into your life.

Another word for grief is bereavement. One grief counselor looked up the old English for bereavement and found it to mean "to be robbed." A family *is* robbed when one of its members dies.

Because grief is a process, it can be looked upon as a journey with a beginning, a middle, and an end. The journey is a long and painful one, and at times it may feel more like a forced march, but you will recover.

Nothing is as exhausting or painful as grieving for someone you love. You will feel tired, worn out. It takes so much effort to walk this road. It is like carrying a heavy, heavy weight, but it does get lighter as you work through your process.

Sometimes people who are bereaved have problems with sleeping. One twelve-year-old boy whose father died found he could not fall asleep in his bedroom any more. So he would go to his brother's room. This was the only way he could fall asleep.

Some people lose their appetite, or, at the other extreme, some people feel better only if they eat all the time. There is also evidence that major losses can make people more susceptible to illness. The immune system's defenses may drop in times of grief.

You may find that your emotions change from one moment to the next. Shock, anger, disbelief, fear, heartache, and depression are usually experienced at different times during the course of grieving. All these strong and painful emotions are steps on this journey to recovery from grief and loss of your loved one. The feelings will come and go. Eventually you will have a feeling of hopefulness toward the future, and you will regain your balance.

Grief is a natural process. Many people expect their sadness and feelings of loss to last a short period of time. However, it is more likely that the end of your journey may be years away. That doesn't mean that the intense pain stays for years, but it may ebb and flow longer than you expect.

Some young people have lost a grandparent or a favorite pet to death, but most of them have not learned how to cope with the intensity of feelings that grief brings. Coping mechanisms take time to develop.

Children and adolescents don't always have the strength to carry the burden that grief brings. Many times you will stop and toss the burden aside. At this point, some kids may seem to "spring back" or get over their feelings fast. This is not really what is happening. When your energy has regrouped, you can pick up your burden again to continue along your journey until your grief is resolved.

"It was so strange. Unreal is a better word, I guess," said Brett, thirteen. "When my mom died three years ago, I would go out and play a great game of baseball and then I'd think that I shouldn't have done that—shouldn't have forgotten that my mother had died—shouldn't have played like I used to."

It's absolutely fine and normal to forget for a while and play that great game of baseball. You need to take "time out" from the pain and get back your energies to deal with it when it comes back again. It's like riding a wave in the ocean. It rises and gets bigger, then it falls and smooths out for a while until it rises again. This is all normal. You can feel the grief sporadically and take rest periods. It's okay.

Many kids try to hold all these feelings inside. They are afraid to let them out.

"I figured if I didn't talk about my father after he died in a car crash," said Tyrone, sixteen, "it would stay like a dream or something. But I held it in and held it in until I almost exploded myself."

Expressing your feelings out loud is one of the best things you can do for yourself. You may feel that you want to tell your story over and over again. That's fine, go ahead. You may need to talk about your mother or father who died and talk about all the things you used to do with him or her. That's healthy. There are many people who are willing to listen and to help you in any way they can. You do have to seek out people to talk to, and ask them to listen to you. If you don't ask, they may be afraid to offer help. They are just waiting for you to show them how to help.

Allow yourself your emotions. Don't hold back on crying, sobbing, trembling, making angry sounds, or even laughing. Pick out the right people from among your friends, relatives, teachers, school counselors, and friends' parents. Many people are good listeners and some are not. Keep trying to find the right people. Don't give up. You can seek out a minister, rabbi, or priest. Often these people have experience in helping a young person deal with the overwhelming feelings that come with major losses.

A very helpful thing you could do for yourself is to find another person your own age who has lost a parent. It helps to know that you are not the only one—you are not alone in what has happened in your life, and sharing your feelings with a friend is good for both of you.

"We named our baseball team The Bad Luck Cubs," said Bobby, thirteen, "because within one year my dad died, Mike's dad died, and Mark's mom died. It comforted me to be with friends in similar circumstances."

Not everyone has had the exact same experience as you, but someone who has "been there" can be a powerful help. You can also be there for someone else. In helping someone else cope with grief, you'll help yourself at the same time. There are groups you can go to in your town, church, or community where the grieving experience is shared. A networking approach can help you through some dark hours. Ask around until you find the right group. The first one you visit may not be the right one. Don't feel strange about not going back. Keep looking until you find one that is right for you.

One important thing to remember is to let your emotions out no matter how horrible or crazy they seem to be. Adults who have had more practice in coping with the stress of loss and grief can verbalize and talk out their anger more easily than young people. Teenagers sometimes can't talk about their pain and are not able to find words for what they are feeling. It's good just to start talking—just start anywhere, say anything, and the words will begin to come.

When you pick up your burden of grief time and time again, you may find your emotions coming out in your behavior. You may find yourself doing things that you've never done before. Some people may act out anger or frustration or grief in school. Your anger at the total unfairness of your parent's death may come out as arguments with your teachers or friends or your remaining parent. Your depression over the empty feeling in your heart may result in failing grades. You may be so exhausted that you may show an "I don't care about anything" attitude.

Fear, withdrawal, guilty feelings—these are the emotions you will have to deal with. Sometimes you may not feel that you can do it on your own anymore. Some people find they need extra help during these difficult times and may seek out a professional counselor or a grief therapist. You may feel stuck in your grieving process and become very depressed. Or perhaps you do feel able to express what's hurting you so much. Or maybe you need support to trust the grief process and where it's taking you. These would all be reasons for getting professional help.

"When my dad died, my mom got to the point," said Rachel, aged seventeen, "where she felt that she was going crazy. She started going to a counselor, who helped her see that she really wasn't crazy. Then Mom took my sisters and me to her too. She helped us learn how to be there for each other but also to allow for our little bits of craziness sometimes."

No doubt some days will be more difficult than others for you. It's important to keep on believing that you'll get through this no matter how hard it gets. Be kind to yourself. Be patient with yourself. Take care of yourself. Keep up with as much of your daily routine as possible, and be careful not to wear yourself out trying to do it all. For a while during the most intense times, you may need to rest or plan lighter activities.

Focus on some physical activities, too. Get plenty of rest. Eat healthful meals and be aware of stress-related reactions from your body such as headaches, nausea, lack of energy, weight loss, and difficulty sleeping. Get medical help if these continue for a long time or get worse.

There are four tasks for you on your journey through bereavement:

1) Accept the reality of what has happened.
2) Experience the pain. *The only way out of the pain is to go through it.*
3) Adjust to the environment without your parent there.
4) Create a cherished memory of your parent who died. The goal is to be able to remember without the pain and fear. This may take a long time.

The grieving process will alter as you get older. There will be significant events and dates in your life when your sorrow will wash over you anew unexpectedly.

"My dad was making a big deal about my high school graduation. I didn't even really want to go," Noah, eighteen, said. "I figured I'd go through it for his sake, but I couldn't figure out why he was so wired up about it. Then when I saw him taking pictures of us walking out on the graduation line, I could see tears coming down his face.

"Then Dad looked at me and said, 'Mom would have been so proud.' I choked up then, too. I had just shut it out that Mom wouldn't be there. It had been six years since she was killed by a drunk driver. I thought I had worked it all out, but I guess it still comes back."

Anniversaries of your parent's death, a birthday, Mother's Day, Father's Day, Christmas, Thanksgiving, and other special days may bring back a rush of sadness. That's fine. Let those feelings wash over you and continue to cleanse the wound. It does eventually heal, that gaping wound you first felt when you found out your parent had died. The scar tissue may trouble you from time to time, and that's okay.

There are some misconceptions about grief. One is that tears are a sign of weakness, especially for men and boys. You may be told, "Now you are the man of the family and you had better start acting like it." Or you may just want to cry and cry and someone may say, "Aren't you ever going to stop crying? This is not really the place to do that." Tears are good, and they are a way of releasing very intense feelings. There is no shame in showing how you feel about your parent who died and the emotions that continue to come up. Tears heal.

Some people don't know how to talk about death and totally avoid the subject with you. Others think that if they mention your parent's name or ask how you are doing, you'll fall apart. So they never mention this huge episode in your life. Maybe you *will* fall apart. And that's okay. The other people can deal with it.

Some people think that if you aren't actively grieving (crying, looking sad, obviously depressed, talking about your loss), then you didn't care very much. *Not true!* Love lasts beyond grief. Don't let anyone tell you how you should grieve or how you should feel.

In the midst of grieving for your parent, it may seem that the bereavement process will go on indefinitely and that there will be no end to the painful feelings. No amount of grieving will ever change the facts of your parent's death or erase important memories. When you allow the process to work, the intense hurt does lighten and you will again feel hope for the future.

If you are the older brother or sister in your family, your younger family members may look to you to help them deal with their questions, confusion, and pain. If your parent is ill and dying, talk to each other about what you can share with your parent at this time. It can be really helpful to be able to tell your mother how much you love her and that you'll all try to be there for each other when times are tough.

It may be that your mother cannot open up about feelings and fears. Try to help all your brothers and sisters talk to your father or another adult who can handle the emotional stress you are all under. It may just be that all you can do is to express your own feelings and fears. It helps everyone to know that the pain of grief is shared.

Maybe you are not much of a talker, and your little brother is asking you question after question because *he* needs to try to find some answers. Help him talk to his school counselor or a trusted adult who can aid him in sorting things out. You don't have to be all things to all people.

If you do wind up taking on the role of counselor—and in some cases you may not feel that you have a choice— remember that it's okay to reach out for help. You are not alone, and there are others who can ease your burden even a little bit. You may find yourself acting as another parent in the family and getting involved in "parenting" the younger ones. It may be a role that is new and different. Do the best you can. Handling that plus your grief takes energy and patience. It will not be all smooth sailing, and the choppy waters that you hit from time to time are exactly like those that happen in any family, grieving or not.

You may need to call a family meeting with your surviving parent and brothers and sisters. You can also ask a close relative to come. This can be a way of communicating about how you will get along. Chores will have to be divided up. All family members will have to pitch in to redefine who does what and when. The leadership may fall to you.

As each member of your family travels his or her unique

path of grieving, support, understanding, and love are vital. No one will follow the same process, and you will all need to allow each other time and space. There is no right or wrong. There are, however, emotionally healthy ways to deal with grief. This book offers some ideas for traveling this road.

You are all survivors. Helping each other and yourself by learning more about death and grieving are ways to help you through this sad time.

There are "stages" of grief that you will go through, and these are in the following chapters. As you work through your pain and are able to resolve your loss, you'll find that you can reorganize your life in such a way that you come out stronger and more aware of life than when you began your journey.

CHAPTER 3

Particularly Difficult Deaths

Having your parent die may be *the* most difficult time of your life. Many of you will have the sadness and pain of knowing that your parent had to deal with a lingering illness. Others of you will have the shock of losing your parent in an accident or some other unforeseen manner. However, there are other ways in which parents die that bring more issues that you might have to face.

Thousands of people die from AIDS each year. This is the disease believed to be caused by HIV or the human immunodeficiency virus. HIV, and therefore AIDS, can be spread to others through sexual contact, the sharing of infected needles by drug users, contact with infected blood and some body fluids, and through tainted blood transfusions.

The people who die from AIDS come from every cross section of life. Arthur Ashe, famous professional tennis player, died from HIV/AIDS received when he had a blood transfusion because of a heart operation. He was a parent.

Craig's mother and father were heroin users in the past. They shot their drugs intravenously with other drug users. Now, years later, Craig has seen his mother waste away from AIDS and finally die. His father is HIV positive but is not showing serious symptoms of AIDS yet.

Neither of his parents were able to work much in the past year. There is no money left. Craig, his younger sister, and parents were evicted from their apartment because they couldn't pay the rent. Now they are living in what Craig calls a "welfare hotel," all in one room with a small microwave oven for cooking, and existing on food stamp purchases. They haven't had any new clothes or shoes for months, even though Craig outgrew his sneakers weeks ago. He just leaves them untied.

At least the room has an old television. That was all his mother could do in her last few weeks before she went back into the hospital the last time. Craig doesn't feel much like going to school, but he goes enough so his father won't get in trouble for his truancy.

What can Craig say when people ask him about his family or where he lives or how his mother died? How does he look to the future when he knows that his father might die too? How does he help his little sister? How does he deal with all this?

Francesca lived with her mother after her parents divorced. She rarely saw her father who moved away. One day they got a phone call from her father's mother, who said that Fran's father was dying from AIDS. Fran's grandmother wanted to know if Fran wanted to see him.

Francesca was stunned. When she asked her mother about it, the most she could get was that her father went to live with another man after the divorce. Her mother didn't want anything to do with him and wouldn't discuss it further. The only comforting piece of information was that her mother had been tested and did not have HIV.

Fran was faced with a heartbreaking dilemma. She decided not to see her father. When he died, she told people he died of cancer. Her grief and shock were clouded by guilt and confusion.

Having a parent die from AIDS adds another dimension to the grieving process. You will be faced with questions to answer and decisions to make:

- How do I feel about AIDS?
- Whom do I tell?
- Do I tell everybody and risk having to deal with other people's prejudices?
- Do I only tell a trusted few who might be able to understand what I'm going through?
- How do I feel about my mother/father?
- What are my fears about AIDS being so close to my life?

With issues such as these surrounding the death of your parent you may be overwhelmed by the complexity of it all. Keeping a private journal may be a good outlet for your thoughts, anger, fears, and confusion. Draw pictures of your feelings using whatever colors you feel best express the swirling emotions in which you live.

When you are ready, talk to someone. Keeping all of this locked away inside your heart will only delay your recognition and resolution of your parent's death. You'll stay stuck in the pain, and it will affect your life and your relationships for a long time.

Murder is another unexplainable occurrence. Brutal rapes, robberies, and other violence many times result in murder. If your parent was a victim of murder, your anguish and rage over what happened will probably be unbearable. There are usually so many questions that aren't answered about a murder, and that's hard to face. So many "Why's?" that no one can answer become part of your life.

How do you feel when you find yourself on the same street where your father was gunned down or near the store where your mother was an innocent victim during a robbery? How can you sort out these raging feelings to see what you can deal with on your own and what situations and emotions will cause you to need help from someone else?

Reach out and ask about finding a support group for families of victims of violent crimes. Being with other families who have gone through the intense grief you are feeling can help you very much. You will hear from other people who have dealt with the frustration and anguish of police investigations and murder trials. You need to work with someone in order to keep things in perspective and not drown in the helplessness you may feel.

What if your parent was self-destructive? Not every human being is emotionally well adjusted.

Cocaine, heroin, and other illegal drugs are being used every day by thousands of people. Others abuse prescription drugs, sometimes combining them with alcohol, making a deadly mixture. How can a person cope when the newspaper prints an article on the front page about a mother's driving drunk and crashing into another car, killing herself and the man and his son in the other car? How does one go back to school after a father's funeral when everyone knows that he was found dead with a needle still in his arm, overdosing on heroin?

At times like this a young person may really feel like

never facing the people she knows. Running away doesn't solve anything.

If it happens to you, grab hold of the strength of your family as best you can and rely on each other to brave this storm of emotions. Try not to spend your energy on wondering what people are thinking or saying. Just remember that you are okay and will find, with the help of others, that inner strength to see your way through this.

Some families do move to another town or state to put sad and disturbing memories behind them. Others choose to stay in familiar surroundings, using the love of others to get on with their lives after a tragedy. Shame, guilt, anger, rage, and extreme pain are all emotions you will have to deal with. For a while it may just be enough to get through each day the best you can. There will probably come a day, whether it is weeks, months, or even years after your parent's death, when you will have to start resolving and recognizing that it happened, it changed your life, but that you don't have to let it ruin your life. You can spend years blaming everything that goes wrong on your parent who died, or you can start putting your shattered life back together again one piece at a time.

Dealing with the suicide of your parent will leave you with many unanswered questions. If your parent had been suffering from emotional or mental illness and made the decision to take his or her own life, you may never come to an understanding of how someone you loved could do this. You may wish you had the chance to relive that last day or week because you feel you could have done something differently. You might think you could have saved your parent from making that final decision, yet you could never really have known what was in your parent's mind and heart at that fateful moment.

One family feels that their father committed suicide because he was physically abusive when he was drunk, which was often. Time after time when he sobered up, he had to deal with extreme remorse at the realization that his car accidents and violent acts could have killed anyone in the family. After his suicide the family went through terrible guilt feelings. They thought they should have been able to change him or prevent his suicide. That anguish lives on until it is resolved and accepted.

Family counseling can be very helpful in these cases. There are support groups through local hospitals or mental health clinics where you and your family can meet with others who have dealt with similar situations. Sharing your grief and confusion and asking how others have managed to live through a time like this can be just that one step you need to help you move a little more easily through your grieving process.

Things to remember:

- You are special and lovable. You have inner strength.
- What your parent does is not a reflection of you. *You* are not the one who caused it.
- You could not have changed your parent or saved him or her.
- In the case of a murder or death in which your parent was an innocent victim, holding onto your rage is emotionally unhealthy for you.
- There are so many people in the world who would love to listen to you and help you move through your grief.

You are not alone.

CHAPTER 4

Early Grief

When someone you love, depend on, and look to as the glue in your world dies, it is the most extreme of sorrows. The grief you feel with this death is intense. You feel numb sometimes. At other times you feel raw, wounded, in anguish, and deprived. Grief gets mixed in with everything in your life— sleeping, eating, going to school or work, relating to other people. You are thrown off balance.

At some point in early grief you realize that you are not prepared at all for this experience. Most likely you have never been taught a class or even a lesson on dealing with the overwhelming feelings of mourning. Perhaps you learned all about first aid and how to take care of yourself when you were home alone when you were little, but no one ever showed you a "How to Cope with Death" booklet. Most young people have never experienced the extremes of having a parent die.

In *The Grief Recovery Handbook* by John W. James and Frank Cherry, the authors write that people are ill-prepared to deal with loss. They point out that when we are young tremendous importance is placed on getting or acquiring things, both material and nonmaterial. There is very little teaching about loss.

As children, we looked for praise from our parents. We tried to be good so that on holidays and birthdays we got the toys that we wanted.

As we grow older the idea of getting things continues to be important because we feel that the more we get, the more complete we are. "If I only had that new bike, my life would be the best!" "If I got all As this year, I'd be at the top of my class and every one would look up to me." "If Jill liked me and became my girlfriend, I'd be envied by every other guy in my class."

So when the opposite happens—if José loses the race for class president, if Joan's boyfriend goes out with another girl, if someone steals Tina's new bike, these people feel that things are out of whack, and a sense of loss comes in.

"Try again next year. You'll win the election for sure."

"You'll have plenty of girlfriends."

"We'll buy you another bike."

You're told not to feel bad and to replace your loss as fast as possible. "Your cat died? That's too bad. Well she was old. We'll get you a new kitten this weekend."

Young people are taught to bury their feelings and replace what they lost fast so they don't feel it so much.

It helps a little, but what isn't helped is your need to face your loss, deal with your feelings, and resolve the sadness or grief that accompanies your loss. If you don't live through all your feelings about who or what you've lost, you're not really ready for a new relationship or a new kitten.

Another message you might get when meeting grief for the first time is to mourn alone—by yourself, alone in your room, not in front of other people. It is true that many other people also don't know how to handle grief, so they may leave you alone, let you "have a good cry" by yourself, and expect you to feel better. You may try this, but it won't help you resolve the sorrow you are feeling.

Avoiding feeling anything is common in early grief. You can deny your loss and try to believe you really aren't hurting that much. You may try to pretend that it doesn't matter that much, you're getting over your loss easily enough. All it takes is a little time and you'll be back to normal soon.

When you are told, "Just give it time. You'll feel better soon," it's as if something magic will happen and all the gut-wrenching feelings will go away. And if they don't go away fast (which they don't), then something must be wrong with you because you can't get over your loss and get on with your life.

People don't know enough about pain and the human heart. People don't know much about grief. So they try to gloss over it. You might turn to your friends to help you with this new thing called grief and find out that they are just as ill-equipped to deal with the sadness as you are.

How many times do others say, "Oh, stop crying now. It's not that bad." Or little kids tease others by saying, "Crybaby." People in general are made very uncomfortable by big displays of painful emotions. You may be told to "be strong," or "pull yourself together." This translates into "Don't show your feelings."

There will be those who do not know what to say to you, so they may make inappropriate comments:

"Be strong for your mother now."

"Well, now you're the man of the house. You'll have to take on the man's work."

"It won't hurt so much after a while."

"Come on, pull yourself together. It's not so bad. At least you had your mother for the time she was here."

"Get hold of yourself."

You'll get mixed messages. People will say they know exactly how you feel. They probably don't. They'll muddle through some kind of comment because they are uncomfortable about dealing with your expression of grief and anguish. People do care, but many of them do not know how to deal with your loss.

You may find yourself in a situation, especially in early grief, when you really need to talk. You hope, even expect, others to ask how you are doing. The strange thing is that many will not want to hear how you are actually doing.

"Hey, Ken, I heard about your dad. How are you?"

"Well, I'm feeling terrible. I have nightmares thinking about my father in that accident. I get so angry at that other driver that I just want to kill him. I've been punching walls and people. I . . ."

"Okay, Ken, hope you feel better soon. Gotta go."

People get scared when they are faced with your overwhelming emotions. So they change the subject or cut you off. Or they don't ask because they want to spare you the embarrassment of crying or getting all emotional in public. This is because very few people have had experience or training in dealing with grief in themselves or others.

Maybe you need to talk about the accident in detail. You need to go over your last moments with your mother in the hospital. Talking about it will ease some of the trauma for you.

You might wish to hear:

"Tell me what happened. I have lots of time."

"I can't imagine what you're going through. Tell me how you are feeling."

"Would you like to talk about your last few days with your father?"

"I'm so, so sorry. How can I help?"

There are those who *can* listen and be of help to you in your grief. Seek them out. It may be your next-door neighbor who was your mother's best friend. Or your teacher whose own father died recently. There are grief counselors and people who have received special training in dealing with the raw emotions that come, especially with early grief. After a while, you'll know whom you can turn to. If you can't find one, ask around. There will be someone who can recommend a wonderful, empathetic person who can be there for you in your pain.

Another piece of advice you might hear is, "Keep busy." You might want to get those jumbled-up, intense feelings out somehow, so running around on a basketball court or pounding a tennis ball can alleviate some of the *physical* feelings. But don't get so "busy" that you avoid dealing with the *emotional* feelings that also need to be nurtured and acknowledged. Avoiding ever dealing with the pain is like rocking hard in a rocking chair. It keeps you busy but gets you nowhere.

In the beginnings of your grief, there may be too many emotions to deal with. Feelings of aloneness, fear, anger, shock, and pain cannot be sorted out, categorized, and dealt with in a logical sequence. They will crop up unexpectedly in any order they occur. You can't separate one and say, "All right, now I'll deal with my anger for a while."

You'll need to take the time to nurture yourself through some of the worst parts. Maybe you need to go for a five-mile run and then have a long, hot bath. Baths and showers are great soothers, and the tears you may shed in them just help wash away a bit of the pain. Maybe you've been getting up at the crack of dawn trying to get all Dad's chores done like mowing the grass, washing the car, vacuuming the house. You've been doing all your things plus Dad's since he died, and you've been busy, busy, busy.

Take one day (or more) to *not* jump out of bed. Stay under the covers for a while; slow down your hectic pace. Think about Dad and some very nice memories you have of the two of you together. Roll the old pictures in your head like a movie and "visit" for a few moments with Dad and your memories. Take time to rest, breathe, feel, and remember. The pain will come up too, but that too is healing. Nurture yourself and your emotions.

One of the emotions that mourners have a tough time with is anger. When you are in pain, it's usual to feel some anger. Say you get up in the middle of the night and slam your shin against the corner of the bed. You get mad, right? Or you trip over the dog in front of your friends, and you get mad at the dog. The bed and the dog didn't do anything to you, but the anger surfaced. When you meet pain, anger is usually a part of it. You try to pin your anger on something or someone else. So when a parent dies, this will happen too. It's normal.

You may be angry at your parent for leaving you, for driving down the highway the night she was killed instead of staying home, for not coming to your concerts any-more, for many things. As you experience it, keep in mind that it's all part of the grief. It's not something to feel guilty about. ("I shouldn't be mad at Mom.") Don't censor yourself for honest human feelings. Acknowledge them and allow them.

You might be angry at your friend for saying the wrong things, for not saying anything at all, and anything in between. You might feel angry at doctors, medical people, God, your family, and others. Anger is like a burning in your heart. Let it out by talking about it, or work it out in physical games or activity; otherwise it will burn *you* up. If you deny the anger and keep it all in, you might get physically sick, have trouble sleeping, get stomachaches, or feel that you have an illness, maybe like the one your parent had.

If you don't deal with your anger but take it out on others, you may lose your friends. They may not be able to handle the raw anger poured on them for something they had no part in.

You might take your anger out on the world—like cutting off that driver who pulled ahead of you. When you feel your anger is out of control, tell someone who can help you before you hurt yourself or someone else.

The pain and anger will be there, especially in the time of your early grief. It doesn't disappear. You need to honor that part of you, knowing that it is a normal reaction to grief.

When you feel the anger and rage well up, think about forgiving yourself for the anger, forgiving your parent for leaving, forgiving the world for being unfair. This can be a step in working through the anger and the bitterness. This begins your healing.

Early grief is raw, numbing, intense, unexpected, and confusing.

CHAPTER 5

Shock, Denial

"**W**had just come home from my grandparents' house," said Keisha, fifteen. "There was a police car in the driveway with its lights flashing. I remember thinking, 'Why don't they turn off the lights? Everyone will think something's wrong.'

"My mother jumped out of the car and ran up to the policeman. She must have had a strange feeling because she asked if something had happened to my father. 'Is my husband all right? What happened to him?' she said. The man walked us into the house and told us that Dad had had a heart attack when he was out jogging that morning and died a few blocks away from our house.

"It sounded so crazy I almost laughed," Keisha said. "He was so strong and healthy. No way! My dad wasn't dead. I wouldn't believe it. I didn't believe it for a long time. Not even after I saw him in the casket, and we had the funeral. I kept thinking I was in some kind of nightmare and that I would wake up soon.

"My friends tell me now that I looked really spaced out, like a zombie, for a long time. I don't remember much of those first few weeks after Dad died."

"Even though I knew it was coming, I wasn't ready for it," said Brian, fifteen. "I was only thirteen, and my mother had been sick with AIDS for over two years. She had been in the hospital for most of the last two months that she was alive. My grandmother talked with my brother and me about Mom's dying, but I guess I really didn't believe that it could ever happen. She was away in the hospital. It was easy to pretend that she was still there.

"Then one day Dad came home from the hospital with my aunt, and they told us that Mom had died that afternoon. I don't remember what I said, probably something like, no, I didn't believe it, and I ran outside. My aunt came out to talk to me, but it didn't do any good. No one could convince me that Mom was dead."

"I still have nightmares about what happened," said Troy, eighteen. "Two years ago my father and I were watching a football game on TV. All of a sudden he went into a seizure and slumped down on the couch. I couldn't tell if he was breathing or not. I called 911, and it seemed like hours until help came. I kept trying to remember the CPR I had learned in school but nothing seemed to work.

"The paramedics tried to revive him too, but they couldn't. They all said they were sorry and that I should call someone. But it was just my dad and me. I couldn't think of anyone to call. I went blank. Numb. I think if someone had asked me my name that night, I wouldn't have been able to remember it."

There are all kinds of feelings that you'll experience in grief. People who work with the grieving process talk about the "stages" of grief. The beginning stage or phase of grief is usually shock and denial.

"No way!"

"I don't believe you!"

"You're lying. My mother's not dead!"

Many times shock is the first reaction to hearing that your parent died. This information is unbelievable. It can't be true. A numbness sets in that may last for hours, days, or even months. It is a normal reaction because you have had an overload of impressions heaped on you at once. A severe and important loss is too much for a body to take in all at once, so your systems signal to each other to shut down for a while. You don't let yourself feel the pain at first. It hurts too much.

Just as the body goes into shock after an accident, so too, the mind goes into shock. Our whole being slips into gear to protect us when we are facing an intense and severe emotional crisis. The mind is protected from feeling the huge impact of our loss. It's almost like being anesthetized; some of the pain is shut off, so that the mind doesn't have to deal with it all at once.

Some young people liken this feeling to living in a fog or a dream world.

"It was almost like the gas or 'sweet air' that I get at the dentist's," said Troy. "I lived. I functioned, but I wasn't really there. I felt so detached from reality. It helped. I don't think I could have stood the pain I felt later on right away in the beginning. It would have killed me."

The numbness doesn't last forever. It is a shelter, a temporary cocoon. You can't predict how long it will take to come out of this numbness. It could be days or weeks. You are saved from experiencing the intense hurt. Some people use it just to get through the worst time. Others stay wrapped up in it for a long time. This keeps them from moving through their grief and experiencing the later stages.

Shock sometimes passes quickly, but denial can last a

long time. For human beings, it is normal and natural to try to avoid or hold off very painful feelings. There is a part of you that knows that you'll never see your mother or father again. There is also a part of you that keeps you from believing it.

There are good things that come from being numb and in denial. You are a little better able to cope with all the details and activities that have to be faced right after someone dies. There are phone calls to be made. Calling up relative after relative, friend after friend to tell them that your father was killed in a car crash or that your mother didn't make it home from the hospital this last time is emotionally wrenching. If you felt all the pain at once and tried to talk to all those people, you probably wouldn't get beyond the first word.

There are funeral services and religious rituals that follow a death that also have to be faced. Actually, getting through these activities and being with family and friends helps get you through the first hours and days. Being numb eases the way somewhat and helps you to function during this painful time.

Many times you remember little of what you did or said in those first days while you were in shock. Sometimes the disbelief and numbness you are feeling are so strong that you cannot remember much of what happened.

"This was pretty weird," Mac, fourteen, said, "but I was really mad at my two cousins because I thought they had not come to my father's funeral. I wouldn't even talk to them for weeks. Finally my aunt asked me what was wrong, and I told her. She said they *had* been there and that one of them, Lore, had gotten me food at my grandmother's house after the funeral. I didn't remember any of that."

One of the few emotions that get through the disbelief, shock, and denial is anger. Masking the sadness and pain of the shock works, but unexpectedly sometimes your anger may come flashing out. This is another way to release the frustration and helplessness you feel when you get the sorrowful news.

"I got really mad at my coach right after my mom died," Sarah, twelve, said. "I was playing soccer and making all kinds of mistakes. I guess I just wasn't with it, and he yelled at me. I got so crazy and angry that I yelled back at him and walked off the field. I felt he had no right to criticize me. Didn't he know I was doing the best I could at the time?"

Sometimes you'll shut off the anger or pain for periods of time to stay oblivious to the loss in your life. If you don't see, hear, or touch anyone or anything, then it didn't happen. Your mind chooses to shut down and deaden your heart and mind to avoid the intense despair that threatens to overwhelm you. By staying numb for a while you can suppress the emotions that hover over you, waiting for you to fall apart.

At the beginning, denial and believing sometimes happen at the same time. No, you are not going insane, even though you may feel you are at times. Bereaved people may look for the person who died even knowing rationally that it cannot be.

"I was walking out of school one day," Janice, fifteen, said, "and waiting all the way down the end of the street was a lady with a car just like ours. She was waiting just as my mother did after school when I needed to go right to my dance class. This happened about two months after Mom died, but I started running for the car the way I always did on Tuesdays. Mom would rush me into the car, hand me an apple and a banana, and tell me to eat as I changed my shoes.

"I *knew* it couldn't be my mother. I knew she was gone, but I ran anyway—it was almost as if I could make her appear by running toward her as I used to do. The strange thing was that as I got closer and saw that it wasn't her, I started crying. I wanted it to be her so badly."

How long you stay with your denial and disbelief varies from one person to the next. Even in your own family, you'll each move through this in different time periods. Sometimes the disbelief returns. It may be less intense than before and catch you off guard. It may be . . . "Oh, I can't tell Dad about the touchdown I made. He's not here."

If, in the first few months or throughout the first year or two, you find yourself holding on to the idea that Dad is going to walk through that door, or that Mom will wake you up tomorrow morning, don't get scared. It's all right to give yourself some temporary relief and comfort from your grief. It's like having a soft cushion to lay your heavy head on for a little while. It's okay.

However, it is not healthy to allow your disbelief or denial to obsess you and take over your life for a long time. You'll be stuck in your grieving process for a long time and find that you are not functioning well in your everyday life. If that happens, ask for help from family, friends, and counselors to start moving yourself in a more emotionally healthy direction.

People who are in these first stages of grief sometimes don't know how to act.

"When I went back to school a week after my mother died," said Jen, fifteen, "I was embarrassed. I didn't want anyone to say a word about my mother because I was afraid that I would start crying in front of the class. I wanted to hide. I was confused and couldn't even remember my locker combination. I didn't want to feel different than when they last saw me. I didn't want people to feel sorry for me."

Another way of coping with the first phases of grief is to keep busy. You may load up on activities and chores and rush from one thing to the next. You may try to fill up your day with so much to do that you won't have time to slow down and look at the drastic way your life has changed. This helps somewhat, but you cannot keep it up for long. You need to rest your body, your mind, and your heart so you can start the healing process. Don't get so busy that you block out reality.

Confusion, feeling like a robot, feeling different may be things you'll experience. Most of the time in the beginning, you'll feel as if you are on automatic, just getting through the day as best you can. Sometimes even that is hard.

Teresa had to go back to final exams after her father died at the end of her senior year.

"I probably flunked all my exams because I couldn't study or concentrate. I don't even know why I went. I should have just taken F's, but I thought I'd try. You know, I wanted to do it for my father and show everyone I was okay.

"I was taking what should have been my easiest exam and I went blank. Absolutely blank. I asked my teacher if I could leave and she said 'No, keep trying and do the best you can.' I guess she was trying to be sympathetic, but I just couldn't function. Nothing would come out of my brain.

"I asked again if I could leave and she said I couldn't, so I got up, threw the exam on her desk, and walked out. I would normally never do that, but couldn't she see that I just could not sit at that desk and take the exam? Doesn't anyone understand just how hard it is to even get out of bed in the morning and come to school? I just want to stay in bed and forget all of this. I can't do it!"

The anguish, the confusion, the desire to disassociate yourself from the reality of what happened and go back to life the way it was before your parent died are all very strong. That's where the numbness helps. It lessens the pain of grieving until you are strong enough to cope with it.

During this time you may also find comfort in sensing an invisible presence. You may smell your father's after-shave weeks after he died. You may think you hear the sounds of your mother preparing breakfast even though it's been three months since she died. This is as normal as dreaming about your parent. When you dream about him or her, your subconscious lets things happen that you heartily wish would happen.

"About six weeks after my father died in a plane crash, I dreamed about him," said Frank, thirteen. "He was standing at the foot of my bed telling me he loved me and missed me and that he would always be around to help me, but now he would be around in a different way than before.

"Some people said it was wishful thinking that made Dad appear in my dream. My grandmother says that maybe Dad's spirit did come to visit me. I'm not sure what I believe, but I felt a little better after that dream."

Even as you work through the beginning stages of your grief, remember that there will be times in the future when the "I don't believe it!" feelings unexpectedly hit you. Your mind tries to sort out the loss over and over again, trying to accept and integrate the reality of death.

It is a long, slow process as you move toward acceptance and face the reality of your parent's death. The hardest thing to face is that this nightmare is real and you will not be able to wake up and have your mother or father back.

CHAPTER ◇ 6

Funerals and

Ceremonies

W hen a person dies, many decisions are made in a
short time. Whether your parent died in a
hospital or at home, a doctor has to make a final
examination to certify the death. Your parent's body is
usually taken to a funeral home or a crematorium. You
and your family have to make arrangements about what
happens next.

Your parent may have wanted to donate parts of his or
her body so that other people may live. An autopsy
(medical examination and testing) might be performed.
There are laws about what happens after a person dies.
The laws are there to make sure that health and sanitary
conditions are upheld, and that the physical remains are
properly taken care of.

Since death is very painful for those who are left behind, each group of people has invented their own way to
recognize the reality of death and to heal the pain. We
have many different peoples in America, because we are

the land of all the world's people; we have many different ways of doing this one and the same thing.

If you possibly can, follow your own family's way and stay close to them—being together with others can help you through the days when thinking is difficult.

Some religions require a son or a daughter to perform certain ceremonies, or say certain prayers, and even though you may not consider yourself a religious person, and not wish to do this, it can help you and others if you follow the ancient rites. They are designed to tell your hurt mind that it is over.

Zeynep and Erkut may go to the mosque to wash their father's body and sew it into a simple piece of cloth. It is over. Mehrman takes sweet oil and performs the ceremony at the crematorium for his mother. He knows then that it is over. So does Mai An, in a different ceremony that is Buddhist.

Charles stands beside the Episcopal vicar and takes a pinch of earth from a bowl. sprinkles it over the open grave, and he knows that his mother is truly gone. It is over then. For Jake, the shovelful of earth thrown down onto the casket after the Jewish ceremony has a reason, and then he washes his hands at the door to his house, and it is over too.

Whatever your family's way, it is designed to help you. Follow it if you possibly can.

Funeral ceremonies are planned to support you and your family and friends and to help you deal with your grief. The reality of your parent's death begins to take hold. Many cultures and families have funeral customs that honor the one who has died and provide comfort and help to those who are mourning the loss of their loved one.

Many families in the United States choose to have a

special "viewing" time or hold a wake, either at a funeral parlor or at home. You might have helped choose the box or casket that your parent will be buried in. Another family decision is whether to have the casket open or not. Some people feel strongly that they want it open so that everyone can say a final good-bye. Others feel that the body in the casket isn't "Mom" or "Dad" and that this is not the way they want to remember their parent.

The funeral directors work with you on these decisions and arrangements. They make sure everything goes smoothly so that you are able to be with others, talk, mourn, visit, and honor your parent. They understand what you are going through.

Mourning is different from grief. Mourning refers to the activities and practices that different people and societies perform when someone dies. Some have church services to mourn the dead, others have ceremonies at home. How long one mourns, or follows a grieving ritual, depends on the family, religion, and culture in which one lives.

Many experts on grief feel that for you who are mourning your parent's death it would be good to be able to see and touch the body, but only if you wish to. It is important for some people to see their loved one a last time—to touch her hand or give her a final kiss. It may help to complete the idea that she has really died.

Not everyone agrees or wants to do this. It might be a scary idea for you to kiss a dead person even if it is someone you loved very much. You might want to remember your mother as a live person.

Funeral directors and morticians work very hard to make the person look as much the same as when alive. Cosmetics are used. Some people may be comforted because the peaceful look on the dead person's face means that the suffering is over. Others feel that the makeup looks too artificial. Sometimes the use of makeup and the attempt to make a person look alive make it harder to accept the death. People say "It looks like she's sleeping. I'm waiting for her to wake up."

This sight is very painful. There's no diminishing that, but it is one of the painful steps taken to start your healing. You may feel comforted years later when you think about that final opportunity to say good-bye. It is difficult, and only you can make that decision. Let your feelings guide you. You may already have said good-bye to your parent in the hospital or in your own way.

Sometimes family or religious customs dictate what happens at the wake or at the funeral. Some religions do not allow an open casket.

You may never have been to a funeral before. Many teens haven't. You may be apprehensive about the idea. How will you handle it? What should you do? How should you act?

Just remember that you may experience a mixture of emotions during this time. You might be glad to see so many people at the funeral home paying their respects to your father, or you might find it so emotionally draining to talk to so many people that you wish they hadn't come. You might feel comforted by the shared meal afterward, or you might resent people gathering together and seeming to "party" after your mom's funeral.

It might help to remember that people mean well and have come to support you. Having people around you who love you helps a lot. It is a time to share, to feel, to remember, to love and allow love into your heart at a time when you are hurting possibly more than you've ever hurt in your life. The religious aspects of the funeral are also meant for support and healing. Religious customs have been around for centuries, and they echo what experts on grief say now.

You and your family may decide to have a nonreligious ceremony to honor your parent. People may speak of your mother or father. You might choose to speak of your love, your memories, your loss. There can be music or poetry. You might have a ceremony but no burial because your parent wanted to be cremated. In a cremation the body is burned and the ashes are buried. Or some people ask that their bodies be donated for scientific research, and there is no burial. In these cases it is usual to hold a gathering of friends and family. The Ethical Culture Society is one organization that can help you arrange this. Hotels will also work with you to arrange a nice room where you can all meet and afterwards eat a meal together.

Whether it is an Ethical Culture Society Leader, or someone from your own family, there will be one person to lead, to speak at the gathering, saying what should be said to comfort and console.

Whatever you and your family choose to do to honor your parent's life and acknowledge his or her final time on earth, you will do the best you can. Each family will have its own special arrangements and ideas about the funeral. Religious traditions and cultures differ. No matter what ideas or ceremonies you have, the important thing is to share your grief with those you love. The funeral is a time to be close to others. Grief shared is grief lessened. Facing your loss through a ceremony or funeral moves you along on your journey of healing.

Your parent may be buried in a graveyard or the body may be placed in a building called a mausoleum. There may be some prayers said and flowers placed on the casket. You and your family may be present as the casket is lowered into the ground or you may leave before this happens.

How you feel and how you behave are not things you can plan or practice. You might say, "I'm not going to cry. I know I can make it through." Then you do cry and get upset at yourself. That only adds to your emotional turmoil. Just *be*. Allow your normal and honest reactions to occur. You won't know ahead of time how you'll feel. If there are things that are a part of the wake, funeral service, or burial that you know you do not want to participate in, talk it out with other family members. Tell them clearly, and give them a real reason for your decision. Remember that they are upset too and may misunderstand. Your brother may want everyone to get up and say something about your father. If this is something you choose not to do, it's okay. Just be aware that intense grief can catch you off balance, and handle it as best you can.

If your parent is buried in a graveyard, you and your family or friends will need to choose a headstone. It usually takes some time for the headstone to be designed and made. Usually the stone has your parent's name, date of birth and date of death, and a few words, or a poem.

MARGARET SANCHEZ
June 21, 1955–July 16, 1995
Beloved wife, mother, sister

You may want to go to the cemetery when the stone is placed at the grave. Some people conduct a small ceremony at this time. Some people like to visit their parent's grave from time to time. Some people visit the grave on a meaningful occasion such as a birthday, Mother's Day, Father's Day, or the anniversary of the death.

What you remember about the funeral may be sketchy, or you may be able to recall vivid details.

"We had a lot of people at my dad's funeral service," Troy said. "I remember lots of little kids because my brother was only six and his friends came with their parents. One friend asked my brother if he'd be in school the next day and my brother said he wouldn't, he'd be off for a few days. His friend said, 'Boy, are you lucky.' I had to laugh a little. That's the way those little kids saw it."

"I went around helping everyone else," said Jen. "I didn't want to feel what was inside me. It was too painful, so I sat and talked to my mom's friends, telling them it would be all right. Then I went home afterward and cried. I guess that's what I needed to do."

Some people feel that young children shouldn't attend funerals. Others feel that as long as children are of an age to understand, they should have the opportunity to say farewell. No matter what age you are when your parent dies, you can have mixed feelings about the funeral, wanting to go and at the same time not wanting to go. Talk about those feelings with someone. Ask a lot of questions about what to expect at the funeral. Try to remain open and accepting of your feelings. Express them and seek comfort from the people around you.

Everyone at a wake or a funeral service acts differently. Some people want to talk about the person who has died, while others find it difficult. There will be those who try to lighten the mood by telling jokes or recalling something funny about your parent who died. You may feel like laughing or you may not. There are no right ways to be or wrong ways to be. There may be laughter and tears at the same time. There may be family squabbling and anger, or there may be peace and sharing. Some people are very uncomfortable about expressing their feelings and they might say the wrong thing. But if their intentions are good, overlook it.

One person may say that your mother suffered so long with cancer that it was a blessing for her to die. You might find that sentiment acceptable.

Someone else might be trying to express the same idea, but it could come out differently. She might remark that it was probably a relief for you when your mother finally died. That way of expressing it could make you angry or upset. Your feelings are your feelings, and you are entitled to them.

The ceremonies and customs that follow a death in any family, religion, or culture are intended as an acknowledgment and honoring of the end of a life. The rituals and expressions of comfort are offered to support those who are grieving for a loved one. Take what solace you can at this time. It is all meant to start you on your path and help you as you begin to heal.

CHAPTER ◇ 7

Middle Stages of
Grief

Feelings ebb and flow as time progresses. This middle stage may be the time of the most intense emotions. It is not a constant suffering, yet it will hurt. Think of being a wave in the ocean. As you peak you may feel momentarily "normal." It could seem as if things are falling into place even though your parent has died. Life can be okay.

Then you crash. Loneliness engulfs you. Bewilderment surrounds you. Sadness follows you. You may feel as if you've hit the bottom of the ocean—it can't get worse than this—and then you go though a break in the waves, when everything feels level. For a short time you feel normal again.

This middle stage of your grieving process brings suffering and feelings of disorganization. The numbness has mostly worn off. The anger erupts now and again. The pain washes over you. Tears come to help you release your pain, express your sadness. You may question constantly why your mother or father died and think about her or him a hundred times a day. This is all part of your healing process. Allow it.

You may feel extreme emotions. Hysteria, bitterness, self-pity, and guilt are going to pop up. Acknowledge them. They come to help you even though you might think that you are losing your mind. You may feel that you cannot cope with these mixed-up, intense feelings. You can. With the help, love, and understanding of family or friends, you can.

"I kept it together pretty much after my father died," said Kate, thirteen. "Then I had to go to a new school. I always got A's before. I don't know what happened, but I just couldn't do math. I couldn't concentrate. I still got A's in the other subjects, but I couldn't get higher than C's and D's in math.

"My teacher didn't really know me. I don't even know if he realized my father had died a few months before, but he kept telling me that I was bad in math and asked if I had always had trouble with it. I wanted to scream at him that I was good at math but that something had clicked off, preventing me from concentrating. It was the worst year I've ever had in school."

On the one hand, you may be keeping your mind busy. Different thoughts will spin around and around in your head. Some will be about your mother or father, others about yourself. There will also be times when you feel blank, spaced out and unable to focus or concentrate on anything. Like Kate, something that used to come easily for you might become a problem.

You may need a lot of attention from other people during this time. You probably need to be comforted, touched, hugged, listened to, and talked with a lot. It may be a new and uncomfortable experience for you to be so in need. You may try to shut it out, yet those feelings won't always go away. They may get worse when you are alone. Then things will even out for a while and you can go on.

Loneliness is very common in bereavement. There's a big gap in your life that your mother or father used to fill. It is natural for you to think that no one ever again can fill that void in your life. Every person you love is special and unique, and not having that person every day may be gut-wrenching. Feeling lonely actually means that you *are* dealing with the death. You are facing the truth in your life—that you will be going on without your mother or father. The intensity of these feelings will lessen as time helps you heal.

"My mom started to date only a few months after Dad died," said, Frank, fourteen. "I was really angry—at her, at her new friend, at my father. I did everything I could to stop her from going out. It seemed too soon, that she wasn't being loyal to my dad."

You may freak out at the thought of someone else coming in and marrying your parent. You don't want another man or woman to take that empty place at the table. It's been hard enough to get used to your single parent; how can you make that mental switch to having a new parent? You may not feel ready. All of this adds to your confusion.

You may be feeling abandoned by your father or mother who died. "How could my father have left me when I needed him the most?" Now that your mother is spending time away from home with another man and his children, or your father is out several nights a week with a woman, those scary feelings of abandonment come up.

Feeling abandoned is one of the most agonizing experiences you'll encounter in your grief. Ideas pop into your head like, "If she loved me, she wouldn't have died." You may go through times when you feel worthless, as if you weren't important enough to your mother, so she left. These are irrational thoughts that crop up. They are just more feelings that you'll have to work through and let go of.

Loneliness may set in when you have to pick up the chores that your father used to do. Being in charge of all the laundry, the yard work, the food shopping, or the firewood may intensify your feelings of loneliness. You may resent the added responsibilities, yet would offer to do them forever if only your parent came back. Loneliness allows people to accept the reality of the death. As you pass through these middle stages of grief, you'll feel a yearning and loneliness as you confront the void in your life.

Depression is a natural part of mourning. When we are depressed, we feel irritable, withdrawn, sad, apathetic, small, and dejected. Not being very hungry and wanting to sleep because of extreme fatigue are also part of it. So much energy is being used up in dealing with grief that there's not much left over for the rest of life.

"I'm so moody," may be true for you in mourning. Up and down, crying with pain and feeling detached and numb are also part of this. It's hard to be positive. It's easier to take the stand, "What's the use? What does it matter?" when you are depressed. You'll feel restless at times and at others you'll just want to sit and vegetate. As time goes on, these conflicting feelings and experiences will lessen.

Falling asleep can be difficult during this emotionally trying time. As exhausted as you are, you may crawl into your bed welcoming the chance to fade out and find yourself staring wide-eyed at the ceiling. Almost everyone who goes through grieving has trouble sleeping. Your mind and heart work so hard dealing with your feelings that you are on overload. Usually you work out some of the day's tensions and problems in your sleep. When you are going through an intense period of grieving, your mind can't handle it all and sleep disturbances result.

Some people fall asleep pretty easily yet wake up often and only sleep for a few hours. It is also common to sleep for many hours yet wake up feeling just as tired as when you went to bed. Weariness seeps into your bones, and you long for a "normal" night's sleep. Now is not the time to take sleeping pills, alcohol, or other drugs to try to get a good night's sleep. Find out about relaxation exercises and meditation that can help you deal with the fatigue. Time will also help you get back on track. Naps and little rest times can help too.

Dreams are a way of working through emotional stress. During this stage of mourning, your dreaming may be affected. You may go through a time when you can't remember any dreams. They may be blocked out. At other times you may find comfort in dreams about your mother or father. It is natural to dream about the loved one who died. It is another step on the path to accepting. Some people are able to say that last good-bye in a dream if they didn't have the chance in real life. It is comforting to "be" with your mother or father again, to feel that you still have some contact, even if it is in a dream.

It's important to keep your energy up. Rest, take vitamins, and stay away from junk food. This is a time when you are more vulnerable to sickness. Your immune system is depleted and tired when you are grieving. Sometimes you may not feel like eating. You may lose weight. Sometimes you may eat more than usual to comfort yourself, wanting to fill up that emptiness inside you with food. You may crave sweets or junk food, but it is especially important now to keep a healthy diet.

Because you feel worn down, you might also have colds more often, or feel weak or headachy. You may imagine you are very ill, thinking you have the same disease that caused your parent's death. Confide in someone and tell them your fears.

Guilt is a very strong emotion that may slip in and out of your consciousness during this middle stage of grieving. You may ask, "Why am I alive and not him?" One boy who was in a car crash that killed his father put a lot of energy into questioning why he had not died too. These questions don't have any answers, so channel your energies into accepting your loss.

You might also feel guilty because you imagine that somehow you were responsible for your parent's death. If she hadn't been coming to pick you up from the dentist's office, your mother's car would not have been sideswiped by that truck. If only you and your father hadn't had that argument, he might have paid more attention to how he was riding his bicycle and he wouldn't have been hit by a car.

Why things happen, why life goes the way it does are questions that can never be answered. If you cannot let go of feelings of guilt, seek professional help or find a friend or relative to talk to. You can slide yourself down into a depression from which you may never recover if you feel that you were the reason your parent died.

These middle stages of grief are intense and strong. You can get through them and emerge whole again even though you feel like you are in pieces for some time. You will heal.

CHAPTER 8

Emotional Roller Coaster

So many feelings jump up and down inside your heart when you are grieving that you may feel as if you're on an out-of-control roller coaster. The short respite when you can catch your breath and feel normal again unexpectedly swings into twists and turns of despair.

When the shock wears off and you begin to come out of the numbness, you will feel the intense impact of facing the fact that your parent has died. This is probably the most painful time in your grieving process, yet it's important to acknowledge it. It's like having a gaping wound in your heart. It's facing the fact that your life is changed forever, and there's no going back.

Anger is a very common emotion that will churn up inside you again and again as you heal. It is a normal part of the grief and healing process, so bear with it. You may be angry with the world. "This isn't fair!" you cry. No, it isn't. But you still have to deal with it.

"I think the hardest thing I had to deal with after my

mother died," said Scott, fifteen, "was how mad I got all the time. My aunt is a counselor, and she kept telling me to punch pillows. But it's not the same . . . you know? I really wanted to punch walls. I wanted to feel the pain in my knuckles so I didn't have to feel the pain inside me. I wanted it to go away and it wouldn't."

Your mother is supposed to live, to have more birthdays, to be there when you graduate from high school. "Why did this happen? *Why me?*" It seems to be a huge mistake. You may feel angry at the whole world because you have to go through this and it seems as though no one else can understand.

"I would get so angry, insane almost," said Cara, thirteen, "when Mother's Day came around. My mother died a short time before Mother's Day three years ago and we were doing cards and art projects in school. All of a sudden I had no one to give them to. My teacher said I could give them to my aunt or my grandmother. I went crazy on her. I ripped them all up in front of my class and screamed that if I couldn't give them to my mother, no one would get them. They took me to the nurse because I was hysterical, and my father had to come and get me. I felt sick and mad at the same time. No one knew what I was going through."

Being angry and feeling hostile are normal experiences when a person is grieving. Don't be hard on yourself about these feelings. Explain to those around you what you're going through, so they can understand that your anger is not directed at them. If you feel too out of control, get help from a counselor or a relative or friend.

Anger is a natural phase in your grieving process. It has been felt by grieving people throughout history. Elisabeth Kübler-Ross, in her book *On Death and Dying*, writes ". . . other cultures have rituals and take care of the 'bad' dead person, and they all originate in this feeling of anger which exists in all of us, though we dislike admitting it . . ."

You may direct your anger at things or at people. Depending on your situation, your type of personality, whether you are a young woman or a young man, you may be horribly mad at God, your parent who died, people around you, the unfairness of things, or the world. It is a natural part of the process you are in.

ANGER AT GOD

"Why did God do this? How could He let it happen?" is a cry of bereaved people. You may be told by caring people that your mother or father was "called home to God," or that "God needs your parent to do His work in heaven." "It's part of God's plan," a well-meaning relative may say to you.

These may not be the comforting words that they are meant to be.

For the most part, this kind of anger is okay. As one priest said, "Don't worry, God is big enough to take care of Himself." What is really happening is that you are releasing your sorrow and rage. It is anger, just anger. You need to let it out because anger turned inward becomes depression and is unhealthy for you.

ANGER TOWARD OTHER PEOPLE

"I was home with my father when he had a heart attack," said Chuck, fourteen. "I kept screaming, 'Why hasn't the ambulance come? Why are they taking so long?' When the paramedics did get there, I yelled and yelled at them that it was their fault that Dad died. I told them they hadn't come soon enough and if they had, he'd still be alive. I know now that it's not true, but it sure seemed true that night."

Sometimes you are angry at people because you feel that they could have done something to change the course of events surrounding your parent's death. You may want to punish someone for your father's accident. You may want to punish someone for how bad you are feeling. You may want to lay the blame on someone. There has to be a "reason" for your parent's death; someone must have caused it.

These are normal feelings. In your shock you are dealing with feelings that many people experience when they lose a loved one.

"I was really mad at the doctors for a long time," said Trish, eighteen. "I wanted them to do whatever had to be done to keep my mother alive. It took a while for me to accept the fact that they had done everything they could. She was just too sick."

People who are involved with dying people (doctors, nurses, paramedics, etc.) sometimes are on the receiving end of anger from family members. They understand what it's about. If you are irrationally angry at people who tried to help, it's okay. It is a normal reaction. As time passes you will get a different perspective on it.

"I was mad at everyone who had a father," Joel, fifteen, said. "I kept on saying things to my friends like, 'If your father had just died, you'd be like this too.'"

You may find yourself looking at someone else's parent and wondering why he is still alive when your parent isn't. Be careful not to judge yourself too harshly when you have thoughts that seem harsh or a little crazy—like hating the teacher who was insensitive enough to make you write a Father's Day poem when he knew you didn't have a father. Or getting mad at your best friend because her mother is there to help her get ready for the prom and yours isn't. Let these feelings wash over you, feel the pain, and eventually it will lessen.

"You know who I hated the most?" asked Jeanine, seventeen. "The people who avoided the subject. I know it's hard to talk about someone who died, but I needed to be comforted. One of my mother's good friends saw me at the mall a few months after she died. I expected her to come up to me and at least ask me how I was doing, but you know what? She just waved and kept on walking past me! She acted like nothing had happened."

It is important that the people you know recognize the trauma you are going through. You expect others to acknowledge your loss and sadness. It hurts when someone pretends that nothing has happened.

ANGER TOWARD YOUR PARENT WHO DIED

"It took me a long time to stop being mad at my father," said Kyle, eighteen. "He went out in the rain on his motorcycle to get some cigarettes and he never came back. He took the curve by the lake too fast, when it was slippery and wet. Why did he need those stupid cigarettes so badly? Why didn't he take the car? It would have been safer. If he had made better choices, he'd be alive today and I wouldn't have to give up the college I want to go to because there isn't enough money."

Kyle felt he had strong reasons to be mad at his father. Wishing that things had happened differently can't change the present.

Holding on to your anger keeps you stuck in your grief

and not on the road to healing. You may have all the reasons in the world to be angry. If these emotions are overwhelming or you feel so caught up in them that you can't seem to let go, look for someone you trust and talk to that person about your feelings.

"My mother was so mad at my father after he died," said Megan, fourteen. "She blamed him for the money problems we have. I guess I do, too. He left us a mess. He had cashed in his life insurance policy and taken out a smaller one, so we barely had enough money to pay for the funeral and medical bills. Then we didn't have enough to pay the mortgage. So we had to move. Now four of us are crammed into this small apartment, and it's easy to blame Dad for all this. But he's dead. So what good will it do?"

Do you sometimes feel like asking, "Who's responsible for all my unhappiness and sorrow?" Do you want to blame someone? The driver of the car that killed your mother? The heart disease that took your father's life?

Forgiving, or just letting go of the need to blame, is a difficult but necessary step for you to take. Focus your energies on feeling the pain and letting it go. You will find the strength to do it. Start gently with yourself.

The anger is something that can be worked through. You can take some steps to diffuse it and find a measure of relief. Some people keep their focus on the anger for months and months. This depletes their energy and contributes to the extreme fatigue a bereaved person feels.

There are ways to let go of the anger. Some people can talk about their rage and anger. There are many willing, empathetic people who will listen. Friends, relatives, teachers, school counselors, and many others are available to help you when you are ready. Give them a signal, a word, "I need someone to talk to," and they'll be there for you. Don't worry about how you may sound; just talk and get it out.

Draw pictures. No one will grade your artistic efforts. Get a pad of paper and some crayons. Pour out your anguish onto the paper. Let your heart unload your pain through the pictures.

Keep a journal or write poetry.

"I wouldn't show anyone my diary from that first year after my mother and then my grandmother died," said Bree, eighteen. "When I look back at all the cursing and screaming I did silently with words, I am glad I had an outlet for all my feelings. I cursed out Mom for leaving me, the doctor who misdiagnosed her breast cancer in the beginning, and my aunt who said that my grandmother had 'joined' Mom in heaven. She thought I should be glad they were together. I wasn't. They had both left me when I was fifteen. I needed them. And my diary heard it all."

Any activity that helps you let off steam is acceptable. Running, jogging, bike riding, swimming, and other strenuous activities will lighten your load. You don't have to be an athlete to help yourself this way. Get a punching bag or shout into a pillow so you can have your privacy. As long as you don't hurt yourself, punch or hit pillows, throw darts, chop wood, or do anything physical. The activity will make you feel stronger and more able to cope with your grief. Otherwise, the pain can weaken you.

Usually this anger comes from feeling powerless over what happened. People feel that their lives are out of control. They feel abandoned.

There will be times when you need to withdraw into yourself to sort things out.

If you can find the little bit of strength it takes, reach

out to someone else. Talk about your feelings of being powerless, insecure, fearful, or abandoned. Someone is always willing to listen. Call a Helpline in your community or city. Empathetic listeners are waiting to hear from you. They can put you in touch with other people who can also help you.

"But I really didn't want to talk," Tova, sixteen, said. "I felt that if I opened my mouth to talk, I would start crying and never be able to stop."

That's all right. Talk, cry, grieve. You can always find a nice person to help you, listen to you, and hold you when you cry. Sometimes you will meet a new person that you can open up to, even a storekeeper, or a librarian, so if you feel that no one you know can help you, look around for a nice person outside of your immediate circle of relatives and friends.

CHAPTER 9

Depression

Helpless. Hopeless. Powerless. Worthless.

Depression echoes with emptiness.

"How can I go on? It doesn't seem worth it. Nothing seems worth it."

Depression is a part of mourning. On your path through your grief you'll feel this emotion time and time again. You may feel that a dark cloud is constantly hanging over your head, and that you will never see the sun again. Often in the morning you'll wish you could stay in bed with the covers pulled tightly over your head and not have to face the world—at least not today. Go away, world. Leave me alone.

Feeling that going to school or work is pointless is part of mourning. So is withdrawing from your friends and feeling that no one can possibly understand what's going on inside your head, inside your heart.

Some days you may cry a lot, unable to stop it. Other days you may wish you could cry but the tears are frozen behind your eyes. The slightest effort may take all your energy. "Why can't anyone see that just getting up and coming to school is the best I can do. It's *all* I can do. I can't think and I can't take tests. Why won't everyone just leave me *alone*?"

You might feel fragile—so fragile that the slightest upset will cause you to crack forever into a million pieces.

Making decisions at this time may seem extremely difficult. You might feel confused and off-balance. Life may seem way off track. A chaotic mix of emotions may burst upon you unexpectedly. Life may seem unreal, as if you are walking under water. You may feel hysterical at times, even months after your parent has died.

Your schoolwork may suffer badly. Concentrate? You may not even remember what day of the week it is. Depression will filter in and out of your life. There will be lighter moments that pop in. Cherish them. Breathe in these "breaks" in your depression. When you see a funny movie, it's all right to laugh until your sides hurt. It's fine to take a break from your grief. It's these respites that will get you through the worst of it.

Be aware. Some people get stuck in their depression for months and months, even years and years. They hold on to that deep ache inside and make it their identity, their friend. When they wake up in the morning they make depression their focus even before they open their eyes. "Where are my horrible feelings today? Oh, here they are." And they put them on like slippers to greet the day.

Some people choose to medicate themselves to blot out depression, but medication just deadens a part of the brain. That's really not going to help anyone feel better. It just prolongs the numbness and prevents people from living life fully. When people recommend drugs, it's usually because they don't want to deal with your pain, and if you're sedated they feel you will be less of a bother to them. Seek out the friendship of people who can take you as you are.

Besides trying to drug the pain away, some people may choose to drink it away. Be aware that the depression and pain do not go away just because you blot them out for a few hours.

Some mourners isolate themselves. You might want to cut off all your friendships and hibernate for awhile. You may make excuses to stay home and not take phone calls. After quite a few tries, your friends will get the message and wait until you get back in touch with them. Then you may feel abandoned—how could they stop trying? Don't they understand? Probably not. That's why it's more helpful and emotionally healthy to keep those contacts open, even on a once-in-a-while basis. Don't cut yourself off from life. You need those friends on this journey.

Some mourners bury their pain in food. They turn to overeating to soothe the ache. Trying to dull the pain with mounds of food causes more problems. They gain weight and feel worse about themselves. Some people develop eating disorders such as anorexia or bulimia.

Some people idealize the parent who has died. They stay stuck in depression. They can't accept the reality of death. They might keep their father's den or room exactly the way it was when he was alive, with his coat hanging in the closet and his pipe on the table half full, as if he's going to reappear and resume living. Moving on does not mean getting rid of everything that was his. It does mean putting things into perspective, so that his absence is acknowledged and honored but not enshrined.

Some people feel that prolonging grief depression is proof of everlasting love, but the person who died would not have wanted this. The person who died would want those she left behind to go on with their lives, remembering and loving her as they do so. Being happy again does not diminish the love for those who are gone.

On the other extreme are those who deny their pain and anger. Some people see it as courageous not to show their grief, and they bury it deep within their beings. Handling grief this way does not help people cope with it and grow stronger. Unexpressed pain does not dissolve on its own. People who do not deal with their feelings may experience even more severe depression and withdrawal later on.

Even when you feel most out of control, you really won't lose your handle on reality. Allowing yourself to experience these chaotic emotions is the healthy way to deal with your grief and depression. Forcing yourself to keep it all in and never expressing the anguish can put you in an unhealthy state of mind.

Still others put off their feelings for a period of time. They delay the grief. It may be that they just cannot face the pain right now and think that it will be easier later on. They hope they'll feel stronger in a year or two, so they try to hold it off until then. Sometimes people hold off the pain and depression in order to just keep on going.

You may have to function and maintain life as best you can because your other parent crumbled under his or her grief and now you have to be the parent for a while. So you hold off dealing with your emotions while you support your surviving parent. Sometimes the young person becomes the parent figure in the family.

Taking on most of the adult responsibilities in your family is not especially healthy for you emotionally. You will probably have to do more, but what happens when you have to do it all? Seek out other adults in your family who can help you shoulder the chores. If your surviving parent is unable to function because of illness or grief, enlist the aid of your grandparents or other relatives to get him or her some help such as counseling. You may not be able to work through your own grief successfully if you are holding everyone else up.

At some point it will be your turn to resolve your pain. You can't hold it off forever. You may feel that you don't care about anything. You may work so hard on controlling your emotions that you become stiff and wooden.

When you shut down like this, you lose your zest for life. That bubbly part of you that enjoys living has burst. You feel deflated and empty. If you do not take steps to start meeting and resolving your grief, your life will go way off track. Instead of looking forward to a time when you can feel better, you may constantly be looking back, living in the past, stuck in what was and what might have been.

Then wham! Something else happens. Another sadness, another tragedy, another loss comes along and triggers the grief that you haven't dealt with yet. It all comes tumbling back, swirling around you like a snowstorm, forcing you to look grief in the face and start to meet it.

When you have unresolved grief, problems seem insurmountable and you will need help in resolving all these hidden feelings.

There are also situations where one may hold on to grief excessively. This is tolerated by others because sorrow engages other people's hearts. It may be seen as appropriate by those who don't really see how unresolved it is. Everyone needs to complete the grieving process.

There may be times when you feel you cannot carry your depression even one more step. Thoughts of suicide may sneak into your consciousness. You may feel that you just want out of the pain, and there seems to be no other way. Your grief *is* temporary. It will not last forever. Talk to someone you trust if you feel there's no way out. There is. There always is.

Depression is not a sign that you are a weak person and cannot hold up. It is part of separating from the parent you loved. It is a time when you have the opportunity to meet your emotions and work them through. There's no easy way. But you, either by yourself or with the help of others, can surmount the pain and sadness. You'll develop greater depth in your ability to cope and survive disappointments and loss as you travel the journey of grief.

CHAPTER 10

The First Year

When you first find out that your parent has died, you may feel as if you have been forced into starting a completely new life. There was a "before Mom died" and now there is an "after Mom died." Just as a baby's first year is marked by a series of "firsts"—first tooth, first steps, first word—so too you may find yourself marking off points in this "new" life with firsts.

The biggest "first" for you might be that this is the first death you have had to experience. How can I get through this? What do I do? How do people expect me to act?

There is no blueprint or schedule for how to get through the funeral or rituals that your family follows. Much of it may be a blur or seem like a dream. You may not remember much of what you do or say. You are on automatic and may need to follow suggestions from your other parent, relatives, or a religious leader.

Another first for you may be that you are involved in making the plans. You may help pick out the casket or what your parent will wear to be buried in. You may be involved in the ceremony by choosing to read a poem or say something about your parent at the service.

"I had never been to a cemetery when they buried someone," said Jake. "The hardest part for me was when they lowered my father down into the ground and we all put a shovelful of dirt on the casket. The thing I remember most was that I couldn't do it at first and by the time I got up my courage, a lot of dirt had been put in there by the other people. I got upset when I looked at all that dirt covering Dad. I wished I had gone first but I didn't know how I would feel."

"Firsts" seem to come so unexpectedly, just as your parent's death was unexpected. Even though your mother or father might have been sick, even very, very sick, you're never ready when death comes.

You can never get ready for death no matter how much warning you may have. Tara had a vivid first—the first day back to school after her mother died. She always liked school and felt good about being there. It was another home to her.

"I dreaded going back to school. I felt so different. I was worried about how my friends would react. Did everyone know? Did *anyone* know? How should I act? What would I say if someone asks me about Mom?"

Most people will feel uncomfortable about going back to school after a parent's death. You may worry about a teacher's saying something to you in front of the class and not know how you are going to react. What if another student makes a remark that gets you upset? How can you concentrate on term papers and history tests when you can even think straight? Your mind is all jumbled up. You worry about crying in the cafeteria.

One way to get through that first day back at school is just to go with your feelings. If you want to act as if things are okay, go ahead. If you feel that you may have some upsetting things happen, go see your counselor or another person in school who knows what happened and can give you a safe place to come and cry, hide out, or get yourself together. The school nurse is often very good for these sort of crises too.

You might feel better if your classmates know what happened before you go back to school. You or a relative can call your school counselor, or principal, or teachers, so you can ask them to explain to your schoolmates what happened. If you don't want anyone saying things to you in front of the class or at all because of how fragile you feel, it is good to communicate that too.

Arranging these things beforehand may get rid of some of the anxious feelings you may have about returning to school after you've taken a few days off.

Some families signal their loss without words, by wearing a black or purple ribbon or armband. This can be a reminder to your teachers and friends to be gentle with you—but arrange it with the school first, since some cultures use quite different symbols.

Another first you will have to deal with is the first Mother's Day or Father's Day without your parent. Some families downplay the day by not giving it too much energy. It may be too painful. You may want to "get through" the day. Other families might try to keep it special. You might go to the cemetery or to a religious service in a place of worship in honor of your parent.

What happens if some members of your family want to forget about Father's Day and others want to make a big deal of it? That's something you as a family will have to decide. And it's better to do it in advance. You and your mother might go to the cemetery, while your brothers may opt to stay home. Everyone mourns in their own

way. You'll need to honor other people's feelings even if
they differ from yours.

The first birthday of your parent after he or she died is
another milestone. You may want to spend time in your
family reminiscing about past birthdays and how they
were spent.

Holidays creep up on you too. The first Id bayram,
Hanukkah, or Christmas without your father—the first
Thanksgiving without your mother to carve the turkey can
be painful. Do you stick with exactly the same things you
did each year, or do you change the traditions somewhat?
If your family doesn't talk about what each one would like
changed or kept the same, then someone in your family
may make a hurtful decision and you may not like it.

Many times families just wing it and get through the
special days of holidays and celebrations as best they can.
Sometimes your pain is increased by not being happy
with the way things go on that day. It is very helpful to
try to set up some plan in advance—who will do what,
which traditions will be continued and which ones will be
altered, etc. This will be the first time you are not with
your mother or father on a very special day. You might
feel out of sync or very depressed. Go with the feelings.
There's no way around the sadness except working it
through. Stay with the pain, and do not run away from
the others until you have settled things properly.

Sometimes the first doesn't come up in that first year.
Chereen came upon her first prom three years after her
mother died.

"I guess even though my mother wasn't here, she was
the one I had always expected to take me to buy my
dress. It was an important day. I wound up dreading it
and avoiding shopping. I looked forward to the prom but I
just wanted someone to put a dress in my closet for me to

take out and wear that night so I didn't have to face shopping without her," Chereen said.

About a week before the prom she knew she had to do something. Her older brother's girlfriend offered to help, but instead Chereen asked her boyfriend's mother to help her choose. She wanted to have a mother figure go with her.

Being without your parent at crucial moments is very difficult for many teens. What about that mother-daughter luncheon your Scout troop puts on? How do you make your way through the father-son camping trip? Can you choose to go with your best friend and her parent, since you feel like her teenager too? This is one way you can deal with this.

The first year without your parent presents many days that you would ordinarily have spent with him or her. Such a day may be as unremarkable as the first barbecue without father or the first game of the basketball season without your mother sitting there cheering you on. It can be a big day, such as your high school graduation or the day you find out about the scholarship to college that you never could have gotten without your parent's coaching or tutoring.

But you do get through these days. You may even surprise yourself when you can look back on the time and see how well you held up. Through dealing with your despair and sadness, you'll grow up learning that you are strong and that you *can* do it. There will be times when you feel like giving up, especially during that first year.

You'll often wish you could just avoid the reminders that your parent is not with you. But as time goes on you'll realize that it's not the first time you did something without your mother or father. It's the second, or the third. It isn't always easier, maybe just a little bit different or less unexpected.

Beyond the first year, you'll meet other firsts—graduations, weddings, perhaps your own first child—which will make the feelings of loss well up again. This is all part of life's journey.

You will wish for a magic formula out of the pain, but that is not the road to healing. You cannot choose to avoid the pain unless you completely block it out. If you do block it out mentally or with pills, it will stay with you, shadowing your life, until you do choose to deal with it.

The best thing you can do for these firsts is to let your family and friends know that you need a little extra attention, to honor all the feelings that the day brings. Sometimes you can decide on your own what would help you get through this special day. Each step you take on your journey on the road to healing will strengthen you and help you realize you *can* get through these tough times.

CHAPTER 11

Religious Beliefs, Questions, Fears

W hen you are faced with the death of your parent, you may question, "Why Mom?", "How could this happen to Dad? He was such a wonderful person," or "Why did this have to happen to me, to my family?" Many people turn to religion as a place to find answers to these painful questions.

You wonder why good people like your parent have to suffer. Questions about what happens after death and whether there is an afterlife may become very important to you at this time. You start looking, searching for a spiritual answer to the pain in your heart and soul.

Many teenagers find comfort in religion. You may get comfort, solace, and a feeling of hope by praying. Just don't get caught up in the "If only's"—"If only I had gone to church or the synagogue, mosque, or temple more, my mother might not have died." Don't beat yourself up like this. You don't get punished by someone's death.

From the moment we are born, we are destined to die. Whether we are young or reach old age, *everyone* dies. Everyone will have someone die in their lives. For you it was your parent, and now you search for answers to ease your pain.

When you are mourning for your parent, others may try to offer you comfort by saying things like, "Heaven is really beautiful. Your dad will like it there," or "God knows how strong you are and that you can handle it." These may not be things you want to hear at the time. It's just that others are trying to offer you peace. Many good-hearted people do not know what else to say.

There seems to be no answer in religions as to why some people die and others don't. Christians believe that the Messiah will return to judge all souls and bring peace, and that the dead will be resurrected and brought to the "Kingdom of God." The Jews are waiting for the Messiah to come, to bring the age of peace. Islam teaches that we close our eyes on this world and open them into another, which is a beautiful garden, and Pure Land Buddhists believe something similar. But exactly what happens after a person dies, only those who have passed on know.

There are many, many religions in the world today. Every one tries in some way to comfort those who grieve. Much of the thought today is that the loved one is not gone, but that the spirit or soul lives on in another dimension. You are still able to love your mother in your thoughts, dreams, and heart. The person you loved will always be a part of you no matter what.

As you keep your parent alive in your heart, your relationship continues. "What would Mom think of my giving this speech?" and "If Dad could see me now, would he be proud of me?" It is in this sense that your parents live on in you. They never leave you. Most children, no matter what age they are, want to please their parents. It doesn't stop even after they die.

Most religions accept the finality of death to the physical presence here in this world. The body dies and is buried or cremated, and yet most believe that the essence, the "soul" lives on. But how and where are more questions to ponder.

Is there life after death? Many, many people search for answers to that perplexing idea. What is it like to be dead? There are many stories about "near-death experiences" in which people have come back to the physical plane after "dying" and leaving their bodies. Many of them speak about following a bright, white light and feeling loved, peaceful, and happy. Many relate that they did not want to return here because the "other side" was so wonderful and inviting. But there is no agreement about what actually takes place.

There are many people who believe in a heaven and a hell. Heaven is thought to be a wonderful, beautiful, peaceful place where good souls go after they die. Hell is believed to be the place of punishment for all the bad souls. Children are taught versions of these ideas as they are growing up. Sometimes as people grow, they question religious teachings. Right now, as you are confused in your sadness, you may question what you've been taught.

After your parent dies you may find yourself believing more in the idea of reincarnation, or rebirth, the soul coming back over and over again, to live in other forms.

Some people believe that there is a life for the soul (possibly reunited with its body) in another world. Jewish ideas include the souls returning directly to God. Catholic thought has souls going first to a purgatory where they are cleansed before they are allowed to enter heaven.

These are ideas from Western religions. In many

Eastern religions, it is believed that we are all a part of nature, and even after our bodies die, we continue as part of nature. There is also the idea that each soul is reborn in a cycle of many rebirths before it can be reunited with the one, the universal spirit, or the Godhead.

Some people try to get in touch with their loved ones who have died. They go to mediums and psychics to establish contact with their loved one. Be very careful if you decide to go to a psychic. Sometimes someone will offer you a free consultation, in order to draw you into a relationship in which you will become dependent on this person. Remember, these people are in business, and they may make false promises or say things that will scare you. If you feel you must satisfy your curiosity about this, have a friend go with you. Your friend can make sure no one takes advantage of your vulnerability.

Many people believe that only the physical body dies, and that the soul or spirit lives on, going on to another realm of consciousness.

Some people who have had "near-death experiences" say they saw a beautiful white light and as they passed through it they were greeted and guided by people whom they had known in their lives but who had died. Many people saw deceased parents, brothers, sisters, grandparents, and other beloved relatives and friends, appearing to be in the prime of life, youthful and vibrant. These people say they now have a different perspective, and they no longer fear death.

Mostly you want to know that your parent is all right, that he or she is not suffering or in pain. Even dreaming of a hug and feeling comforted by your parent eases some of the pain and feelings of loss.

What you have is today and tomorrow, and you can be sure your parent would want you to live for the future.

You cannot go backward into the past to relive it or change it, but you can cherish the experiences that you had with your loved one.

In everyone's life, it is important to move on. To live means to go forward. Be careful not to stay plugged into questioning "why" and fail to move through to a resolution of your grief. Learning from each experience is what makes us grow, and death can be one of the great teachers you may have. You will explore feelings inside you and in others that you may never have known existed or ever met before. The insight and understanding of human nature, yours and others, can be gained in enormous amounts as you experience grief. You will discover inner strength as you cope with and resolve the loss of your parent.

You do not have to be a super-person to deal with it. Just be you, handling it the best you can, getting help when you need it, and working it through. You should let your emotions out, share your grief with the others who are there for you, and always remind yourself that the loved one you lost would want to know that you were coming out of your grief and beginning to live fully again.

CHAPTER 12

Living with Your Single Grieving Parent

L iving in a one-parent family can bring ups and downs that you never thought you'd have to face in your life.

"I supported my girlfriend all through her parents' divorce," said Todd, sixteen. "There was a lot of fighting and anger. I'd listen to her and help her over some of her sadness.

"But when my father died, I felt differently about Aisha's losing her father to divorce. I mean, at least she had a father. She didn't understand my grief. I wanted to die because I was hurting so bad, and she'd tell me to snap out of it.

"We broke up soon after that. I not only lost Dad, I lost my girlfriend—someone that I thought I could turn to when I needed help. She really let me down."

Now you and your family will have to consciously re-structure your family life. Dealing with a grieving parent will take a great amount of patience and support. That's hard to do when you yourself are in so much pain you can hardly function. You see your parent hurting, depressed, crying, not functioning, and you feel helpless.

All kinds of fears may crowd into your head. You may worry about how your family is going to cope with this new situation and all the mixed-up feelings.

"I was really afraid that my father wouldn't be able to handle things," said Ryan, fourteen, whose mother recently died. "I thought our house would fall apart—that my father didn't know how to cook and clean. I mean, Mom always kept track of what we needed. I thought we'd be living in chaos."

Actually, for a while Ryan's family did live an unsettled life. It took him, his father, and his younger sister a few months to get organized into a system that they could all live with. It wasn't the same as when his mother was alive, but they divided up the chores, his father took on more food shopping and cooking, and they survived. They also got closer because they had to rely on each other more.

"When my father died, my mom and I got scared," said Cathy, eleven. "It gets so dark out where I live, and without my father around, I didn't feel safe. What if someone broke in? What could my mother do against a burglar?"

Cathy's mother wanted to move. She didn't feel safe either. She also got so bogged down in her grief that she forgot things like locking the door or leaving the outside light on for her when Cathy came home late.

"I really think my mother lost her functioning for a while. She couldn't think straight about anything. She'd forget to come pick me up, and when I'd get a ride home I'd find her sitting in Dad's chair crying. I wanted *her* to make things safe for me, and she couldn't. I didn't know what to do."

One of Cathy's teachers saw what was happening and helped Cathy and her mother. They asked her uncle to hook up outdoor lights that went on by themselves when it got dark. They persuaded her mother to get some counseling and arranged for a neighbor to stop by when Cathy wasn't home.

When a parent has died many young people begin to feel unsafe and unprotected. If safety is your worry, look into installing an alarm system, and post emergency phone numbers for the police, firehouse, and medical help near the telephone. You can even have a police officer come to your house to discuss with you how to make your home safer.

"It took a long time, over a year, before Mom was able start functioning again. I was scared for all that time. Nothing was the same. *Everything* had changed. Now, almost two years later, I'm beginning to feel safe again."

Time. How long will it take for your parent to get back to "normal"? Will your parent ever be the same again? Who is this new person your mother has become? How many weeks or months will it take before you all feel better?

There really is no knowing how long it takes to work through grief. You may be able to do it a bit sooner than your parent. You may find yourself becoming the parent for a while. Look upon it as a temporary need that your mother or father has.

"My father stopped going to work for weeks after my mother died," Mia, fourteen, said. "The bills started piling up, and all he could say was that he didn't care—that nothing mattered now. I didn't know what to do."

In this situation, don't try to do it all. Get help from someone you trust. Call upon a relative, friend, grand-parent, aunt, uncle, or any other sympathetic adult. Your dad may need help, and you have to be careful to select a very understanding person to do this. Make sure the person is not harsh or judgmental. Take over the chores the best you can, and leave dealing with his employer to an adult. Lean on outgoing people to get you and your dad through this very difficult time.

What worries young people is how to deal with un-certainty. "Can my single parent take care of me?" As time passes you'll see that you'll be able to answer yes to this question.

If your father or mother wasn't the major cook in the family, you might worry now about what meals will be like. There are many easy-to-follow cookbooks and books on nutrition to guide you. Simple meals and a joint effort on your family's part will quickly lead to delicious meals together.

The emotional aspect of sitting down for meals may be hard to deal with. "We all sat in the same seats at our kitchen table," Talib, fifteen said. "After Dad died we'd sit there in silence feeling the emptiness of his chair. It made me feel too sick to eat sometimes."

After a week or so, Talib's older sister asked the rest of the family if they could take the empty chair away, turn the table around, and have everyone change seats. Talib's mother didn't want to do it. She wanted to keep the empty chair there as a reminder, but her kids convinced her that it would be better for all of them to make some changes.

Everyone has a different way of handling sorrow, and you and your family have to work it out so that you don't cause each other any extra unhappiness. You may want to watch the videos of your mother's last birthday party, but your father may not be emotionally ready for that. Talk it over. Be sensitive to how other people deal with their grief. Try different approaches to lessening the pain.

Lack of money can be a problem to a teen who has lost a parent. Not having that paycheck you can count on can be scary.

"When my father died, he was making twice as much as my mother," Adrianne said. "Now she's working three jobs to pay the bills. She's never home, and I have to take care of my younger brothers. I don't like it and neither does my mother, but what choice do we have?"

Sometimes there is no choice. Wishing things were the same or raging against the unfairness of life will only get you bogged down in negative feelings.

When a parent dies, you may be entitled to receive money from Social Security. If your parent worked and paid into this government fund, you are entitled to a monthly check based on his or her earnings. Look up in your phone book the number for the Social Security Administration office closest to you. You will need to provide information about your parent, as well as your social security number, date of birth, and other data to process the claim. It's worth the time and effort for the paperwork because you'll get a check for each child in the family until you are all eighteen years old. This can help offset some of the financial drain on your surviving parent.

It's also possible to obtain food stamps, if your family income is not sufficient for all your needs. You may even look into welfare to get help with the rent.

If money is one of your main worries, it's okay to talk about it, because the more you know, the less helpless you will feel.

- Was there a life insurance policy or some other inheritance, or are cutbacks going to be a reality?
- Does your mother or father need to take on an extra job to pay the bills, or is there some other way to make ends meet? Perhaps your taking on a part-time job can lighten the load.
- What kind of insurance does the family have now? Is your medical coverage enough, or do you and your parent need to look into a better policy?
- Are there any savings for your future?

If your family has open discussions about money, you'll get a better idea of what you can and cannot afford.

"My mother wouldn't tell us anything," Renee said. "I knew there was insurance money, but we never saw it or heard about it. Mom hoarded it, and I didn't have new clothes to wear to school. We asked and asked, but she wouldn't tell us."

It may be that Renee's mom was feeling so insecure that she hung onto that money in order to feel safe. Grief does different things to different people. Your grieving parent may not always act logically or rationally. Be understanding and learn to live with some of these irrational episodes. Try to ease into a conversation when your parent may be ready to see things more clearly.

"My mother was so afraid she'd get sick and lose her job that she wouldn't spend any of my father's insurance money," Omar seventeen, said. "I tried to talk to her about using some of it, but she wouldn't hear of it. I got a job at a local store so I could have some spending money.

That way I didn't have to bother my mother and she didn't have to use the insurance money until she was ready."

Another thing you'll need to work out is what to do in case your parent gets sick. This may not be something either of you wants to bring up right away, but every family should have an emergency plan. Talk about who would take care of you and your sisters and brothers. Work out together whether a relative or friend would come to your house to help you, or whether you would go and stay with them. Ask about what bank accounts you would have access to in order to pay the bills and have spending money.

If there is no insurance, ask your mother or father to get whatever is necessary to cover all of you medically. Hospital and doctor bills can add up when you don't have insurance. It can be especially tight if your family income has fallen off too.

Part of dealing with your grieving parent is dealing with your own grief. It's hard to help someone else when you need help yourself.

"I really needed to talk. And I mean *talk* about Mom's death," Jackie, sixteen, said. "And Dad wouldn't talk. He shut me out. I wanted to make him talk but no matter what I tried, he wouldn't talk. I was hurting so badly and he shut me out."

Get involved with other things and other people when you feel you are hitting a brick wall with your parent. Nurture yourself, talk to others such as a counselor, a teacher, a relative, or a friend who can listen sympathetically. Even if all you really want is to break through that barrier your father has put up, you may have to back off for a while. It could be weeks or months before you can get your father to open up to you. There may be teen grief groups in your community where *your* needs can be met and you can find some nurturing.

Some friends may avoid you because they don't know what to say to you. They could be nervous and not have any idea of how to help you. You can bring up the topic. Be open and matter-of-fact about it. This will make them feel better about talking it over with you.

Try to get help from your parent. If neither your mother or father are ready to reach out, you can ask to have a few friends over from time to time. Your parent may object to what seems like a party, so you'll need to communicate that being with your friends is soothing for you.

Bringing out into the open your worries and fears to your parent will help him or her tune in to what you are feeling and where you are in the grieving process. Try not to shut him out. Work with her in solving the day-to-day problems. You may find that your role in the family changes, probably a little, possibly a lot. If you're not sure how much responsibility you should take on, talk it out with the rest of your family.

At home, you may feel that you have to shoulder too much responsibility. Instead of being angry, com-municate. Even when you are dealing with the toughest pain and anger that you've ever felt in your life, reach out to your family and talk. Your mother or father needs to recognize your needs. Maybe before you go to bed you could ask your parent to come into your room and have a talk the way you used to do when you were little. If you feel you can't talk, write a letter.

Every family's situation is different. Try to put your energies into helping everyone deal with the grief. It's hard to predict how your grieving parent will act and react. Maybe that's the only thing you can count on—that there's no right or wrong way to deal with the pain. Be understanding, share your own feelings and needs, commuicate about family responsibilities, and reach out to each other. Keep that bond strong. You and your parent will make it through. You can survive this. You will grow and find strength you may never have thought you had. Keep the love flowing.

CHAPTER 13

Upheaval and Changes

Facing the changes that happen after your parent dies is a challenge. It's a challenge that you'd rather not have in your life. Not having a choice may make you feel helpless and angry. Spend time with these feelings. Get help to work them through. At some point you'll realize that life means change no matter what. Of course it's hard to welcome change when you are hurting and grieving.

MOVING

"It was like a bomb shattered my life." said Justin, sixteen. "Six months after my dad died, we had to move. There was no warning, no nothing. Mom said there was no insurance money, and we couldn't keep the apartment. We moved to another town, to a smaller apartment. I had to go to a different school and I didn't know anybody. It was awful. I hated it."

Moving may be one of the problems you come up against when a parent dies. Not being able to pay the rent with your surviving parent's salary may be a reality.

"I'm not going!" may be your first reaction. It's hard to move, no doubt about it. You've been close to your girlfriend for eight months, and she's also helped you though your grief. How can you leave her? Moving away from close friends gives you a sick feeling. You're finally starting on the school soccer team. How can you begin at a new school?

If you can accept that you have to move, then you can turn your energies to making it a positive experience. You can start over in school and maintain your friendships. Here are some helpful hints for making the move better.

MAKING FRIENDS

The hardest part of moving may be leaving your friends. You've been grieving, and now you face another loss. Your heart may feel broken, and your feelings of grief and loneliness may intensify. Dwelling on the pain could bog you down. Instead, make plans with your friends to visit each other, to write, and to call. Don't leave this important step undone. Make definite plans so that you won't drift apart. Look at a calendar together, and write things down. Give each other phone numbers of relatives and friends in case you are temporarily without phones, so you won't lose each other.

Susan's mom moved the family three states away to be closer to her grandparents after her father died. Since it was summer, the first thing she did was find out where the local pool was. That's where she made her first new friend.

Go to the local library to see if enrichment classes for

teens are being offered (an astronomy club, a journalism workshop, etc.). Volunteer to help out reshelving books in the town library—that's where lots of families go weekly.

"I got a job in a clothing store in the mall in my new town," Carol, sixteen, said. "I knew I had two choices: I could hang around home feeling sorry for myself, or I could make an effort to start over. I met new people right away, and of course, the money helped. My mother has had a hard time making her paycheck cover all our expenses. That's why we had to sell the house and move in the first place."

How about your new city's recreation area? After Joe moved, he signed up for tennis lessons at the park. After a few weeks he entered a doubles tournament, and within a short time, he had a nice group of new friends.

Work up your courage and approach other teens at a soccer game, or at a meeting of the local environmental club. You may have to be the one who speaks up first.

"I was really shaken up after my mother died," said Jason, fifteen. "Then we had to move. That was terrible. Packing up and cleaning out all my mother's belongings was so hard. But when I got to my new neighborhood, I knew I would have to make the first move toward new friendships. I forced myself to walk up to someone and start a conversation, and it worked out fine."

You'll always think of what you left behind when you move—your friends, the family life you used to have, the security you felt. Your parent who died and your old friends will always be a part of you.

In a short time you will find new friends who will enrich your life. You've been given the opportunity to broaden your circle of friends. Each has special and unique gifts for you.

DISCOVER A NEW LIFESTYLE

Maybe you have moved from the country to a large city. Get out and walk around. Find all the museums, the art galleries, the zoo. Explore all the stores, boutiques, playgrounds, and recreation areas. Something is always happening in the city, so you'll never be at a loss for things to do and discover. Look in the newspapers and on library bulletin boards for interesting things to do.

"The town where I used to live was pretty big," Jeff said. "But when I moved here I was scared. This city is huge! Then my older sister and I decided to walk around and explore different neighborhoods. We found neat things to do."

Perhaps you have left that big city where you could walk or take a bus anywhere you wanted to go and now find yourself in a rural area.

"I liked where we lived," Kelly said. "Dad and I argued a lot about moving back to the town where he grew up. I know he wanted to be closer to my grandparents because he was so upset after my mother died, but it didn't seem fair. In the end I had to go, dreading the move."

You can make it a positive experience. Plant a garden, learn to ride a horse, breed rabbits, become a long-distance runner, explore the countryside, and find the recreation areas.

"Living in an apartment for most of my life meant never having a backyard." said Cassie, fifteen. "When I saw all this land, I decided to grow flowers. I never knew that I had a green thumb until my garden blossomed. I also put my dad's favorite statue in the middle of it, as a dedication to him. It helped me feel close to him, and more at home in this new place."

Maybe you've always been a Sunbelt person who now has to brave the cold New England winter. Learn to ski or ice fish, or get a job tapping maple trees. There are always new adventures to enjoy in a new place.

STARTING IN A NEW SCHOOL

Going to a new school is tough. You've left behind the familiar, the comfortable, the enjoyable and headed for the unknown. There are things you can do to make the transition a little easier for yourself even though you may not feel enthusiastic at first.

If you move over the summer, register early for school. Most schools prefer that you don't wait until the very first day of school in September to choose your classes. Sign in early in August if you can, and bring last year's report card and your immunization records.

Ask for an outline of the courses offered, and if you have any career goals at this time, discuss them this time with the guidance counselor. If you don't have your records, make a list of the classes you've taken and the grades you received for the past few years. Select the correct level and make sure you know what the graduation requirements are. Your old school may require two years of math to graduate while your new one wants three.

Ask for a student handbook with all the rules and regulations, and a map of the building so you can take a tour through the halls to familiarize yourself with the guidance office, the nurse's office, bathrooms, cafeteria, gym, and library. Find out about bus schedules, driving regulations, and alternate transportation to and from school.

Inquire about clubs, sports, school newspaper, yearbook

staff, and other after-school activities. Volunteering to help in the front office or library after school may be a nice way to ease into a new school situation.

Take advantage of what the new school has to offer. "My old school had only a few clubs," Stacy said. "But here I joined the ski club and work on the newspaper."

Jon was somewhat shy in his old town, and he often wished he could change the way others saw him. In his new school, Jon decided to be more outgoing, and he tried out new ways of approaching people. He gained confidence and began to overcome his shyness.

Talk to a school counselor about your background. You might not want your new schoolfriends to know that you just lost a parent. It may be too painful for you or you may be afraid you'll burst into tears if you start talking about it. It's all right to confide in someone. A teacher, a counselor, or a new friend can help you break the ice and talk about your loss. You may feel that no one can understand what you feel or what you're going through, but you just might find the right person who can be there for you.

"My father died a week before my senior prom," Teresa, eighteen, said. "It was also three weeks before I graduated. I had to go to Awards Night and accept the two scholarships I had won. I was numb for most of that, but one morning during my final exam in history I just couldn't do the map section. I blanked out and felt like I was going to explode—I was all full of crazy, mixed-up feelings. My teacher yelled at me. I got up and walked out. I usually don't do that. But I just couldn't stay there."

Fortunately for Teresa, she knew that she could go to one of the vice principals, whose husband had died two years earlier.

"No one understood how hard it was just to get out of bed and go to school. Then I had exams on top of that. I was really upset. I went to Mrs. Cooper, and she knew exactly what I meant. She said there were days when she felt paralyzed and just wanted to stay home under the covers and hide from the world. That's what I was feeling too."

MOTHER OR FATHER DATING OR REMARRYING

At some point your parent may begin dating again. You will probably have mixed feelings about this. On the one hand you might be able to see that your mother wants to spend time with a man, yet on the other hand you may be angry or hurt that she is trying to fill the void left by your father's death. You may feel your father is being disloyal to your mother's memory by dating someone else. You may think it's too soon or not right.

It might help you to remember that each person deals with grief in an individual way. It may be too soon for you to try to imagine another man at your dinner table or unwrapping presents on Christmas morning, but your mother may be ready for a new relationship. Your sister may be happy to have another "mother" in the house, but you may not. You are all working through the acceptance of your parent's death and you may all have different reactions to someone else coming into your family.

While it isn't up to you to tell a parent that he or she or cannot date yet or get married again, you should talk about your feelings. Good communication is the key to understanding each other's needs. Expressing your concerns, worries, and fears in calm times does more for your family than yelling out your objections in the heat of an argument. Death brings change to your family. Change cannot be stopped.

"I really hated this woman my father was going out with. She had two other kids who visited us, and we had to share our rooms with them," Sandra said. "I spent the first year and a half being mad and trying to break them up."

In the long run, Sandra and her family worked things out. They got more and more used to each other, and she began to accept the idea that her dad's fiancée could have a place in her life. "Instant" families don't happen. Working though issues and giving time and space to a new family unit will help you all get on a stronger footing. Try to see how you can find some positive effects in new situations.

LIVING WITH GUARDIANS

When a young person is suddenly without parents, she or he must find out immediately if there was a will. Often, the will spells out the parent's wishes for guardianship.

If there is no will, and no money, the state in which you live has a process to help you find a foster home.

If your parent left any money or property, you will probably inherit the estate (whatever was your parent's). In the will, your parent usually directs the executor (the person who carries out the wishes of the will) to create a trust fund for you. This means the money, insurance money, and property are held for you. You cannot always get all this money right away. There may be a trustee who regulates how much money you get each month or year. When you reach a certain age, you will probably get the total amount left.

Some parents die without leaving a will. If there is no will, it takes the courts to work it all out. It is much more difficult this way, so it is important that parents write wills. Your life will be a little easier if your mother or father left plans for you in the will.

Usually a guardian will have been named for you in your parent's will. If not, a relative can step forward and assume guardianship. If your mother or father has remarried, you may choose to form a new family together. There can be all different kinds of arrangements here, and each one is unique. The most important thing to focus on is that your living arrangements will change, perhaps a little, perhaps a lot.

The least amount of interference with your life would be if a guardian could move into your home with you. This might be too difficult to arrange. Most likely you will have to move into a new family arrangement. It is said that you never truly know another person until you live with him or her, so even though you may know your grandfather, or aunt or uncle well, keep an open mind about new things you will discover about that person. There will be new house rules and procedures to discuss and negotiate. Different chores and responsibilities will fall to you. You may have to share a room, even though you prefer having your privacy. A different family, maybe a different town, state, even country, will all be added to your grief.

What if you have brothers and sisters? Where will you all live? Ideally, arrangements will have been spelled out in your parent's will and hopefully you can all stay together. If you have to split up and live with different relatives, sit down together and make plans to keep constantly in touch and work toward seeing each other as often as possible.

When it seems that your family is being shredded apart, there are things you can do. Keeping in touch by phone, letters, and visits will lessen some of the pain. One teenager found herself sent out of state while her two younger brothers had to move to an uncle's house. She put all her energies into keeping in touch with her brothers and waged a campaign to find a place to live in their town.

As her brothers told people about her, miracles came to pass. One of the boys' teachers had an extra room in her house, and after much planning and eliminating of obstacles she was finally able to move in with this teacher, who became her legal guardian. It wasn't easy, and it took almost a year to accomplish, but she did it. She now sees her brothers almost every day, and they won't ever forget that they are family. She wouldn't let this happen.

At times much of this will be overwhelming. At first, you won't have many choices. For the most part, you may have no choice whatsoever, and that alone may add to your feelings of powerlessness and despair. How do you cope? How can you deal with facing a completely different life while you are still reeling from the death of your parent?

This is the time to reach deep, deep inside yourself for the strength to make the best of things. It isn't what you ever planned for in your wildest dreams (or nightmares), but you are faced with it. There are some things you can do to make it the best it can be, and in many instances, it won't be as bad as you are afraid it will be.

Try to bring things from your old life with you. Hopefully you can bring your dog or cat or whatever with you so that at least you have one "member" of your family with you during these changes. In your room, or your half of the room, hang your favorite posters and pictures on the walls. Bring your stuffed animals, sports equipment, family photo albums, and cherished possessions into your new life. They will all have a place there to comfort you and build the bridge to your future.

Try to do the things you're used to doing. If you used to have a cup of tea with your mom after dinner and talk about the day, see if you can create that again with your guardian. It won't be the same, but the familiar ritual may help. You may decide after trying this out for a while that it's not working, and discard the idea. It's all right to experiment to find things to do that will comfort you and make you feel less strange and out of place.

You might be fortunate enough to feel right at home where you are living now. Cherish those feelings and use them to soften the grief that will engulf you unexpectedly. It can never be the same, but it can be made a new home if you are able to leave open the opportunity for accepting change.

This acceptance may take some time. You probably will also have to grieve the loss of your home, family life, routine, familiar places and things. You can feel great anger and hopelessness at the changes and upheavals in your life. If your guardian is an open person, talk to him or her about what you are feeling. Chances are he or she is also reeling from the quick changes and adjustments it takes to have a new member in the family. Understanding, communication, time, space, and *love* will see you through this difficult time.

If you have no relatives with whom to live, you may become a ward of the court and be placed in foster care. This is a government system that finds homes for children and teens who have no other family. You may live for a short time in a group home, or in a shelter or temporary placement, while a permanent home is being found for you. There are many kindly families who take in foster children, and the local government has special people whose job it is to put you in touch with them. This person is called a foster care worker.

You will have a foster care worker assigned to you who will be responsible for your placement and welfare. You must keep a line of communication open with this person. In the past it was your parent who looked out for you and took care of you and your needs. Now you'll need to do this for yourself by making yourself known to your caseworker and keeping this person up to date on your expectations, what you need, your goals and aspirations, and your desires.

Your counselor or minister, priest or rabbi can also be of great help to you in the foster care system. Discuss everything you need to with your new foster family and your caseworker. Ask for the help you need in dealing with your feelings and your life. It takes practice to do this, but you are not alone, although at times it may feel that way.

Upheavals and changes seem to come one right after another when a parent dies. No one is prepared for them; you just have to do the best you can. Try to keep in touch with the love you had for your parent who died. Most of all, love yourself. This is definitely not the time to put yourself down in any way.

Reach out to others. Talk. Explain what you're going through. You may have to learn how to do this—just keep on trying, and don't give up. Ask someone to listen. Let someone help. As alone and isolated as you may feel, there will be someone out there whom you can count on. Just hang in there, one day at a time, and you'll make it.

CHAPTER 14

Counseling

Elena wound up in the school nurse's office.

"I just couldn't do it any more. I tried and tried to keep it all in, but I couldn't. It just comes bubbling up all the time and won't go away. I need help."

The "it" that Elena is talking about is the mixed-up, confusing emotions that accompany the grief process. You can only keep a lid on it for so long and then "it" erupts, taking you by surprise in the middle of chemistry class or out on a date.

The positive part of Elena's experience here is that it has brought her to a point where she can acknowledge that she cannot handle her pain alone anymore—that she needs someone to help her. If you reach that point also, there are people who can help you. Sometimes they see your need first, but usually you must reach out to them and get involved in counseling in this way. There are trained, professional people who are there and who can help you.

Where are they? How do you find them?

There are services connected with any hospital, which includes group counseling for grieving people. Most of the churches, synagogues, mosques, and Ethical Culture Societies have bereavement counseling on a regular basis. You can also call the community services department at the hospital in your town and just say simply, "I need your help—please help me." There will be a person who arranges for widows' and widowers' groups, teen grief groups, and art therapy/grief groups for younger kids. You should be able to make a start there. If the hospital doesn't have a group going on right now, the person there will be able to give you other contacts you can make to find another group.

Try also within your own school. It may not seem that other kids have gone through what you have, but there are. See if your counselor or a caring teacher is willing to lead a grief group for a short time. Six to eight sessions is sometimes enough to help lift that burden you are carrying in your heart and give you the opportunity to look at your experience in a different way.

You can also get some help from the people who work at funeral homes. They are trained and have experience that enables them to tune right in to what you are going through. They may come to your house or talk to you on the phone to help ease you through your most painful times.

Counselors who have private practices can be another choice for you. If you don't know where to start finding the right one for you, it's okay to ask around. In your school guidance department you can ask for information on someone who helps with grief counseling.

Ronald Keats, a psychotherapist in private practice, has worked with teens in the field of bereavement or grief counseling. He stresses that teenagers may be helped to tune in on the memories of the parent who has passed away.

"Even though their loved one is physically gone, the teen can concentrate on the spirituality of the parent who has died," Keats explains. "Concentrate on poignant memories: their mother's perfume, the advice she gave, how she dressed, the father's after-shave, the smell of his pipe, the activities shared. The more you can get the teen to realize that he has these memories ingrained deeply, then he can know that he is never without that parent."

"The clearer the memories, the stronger the spiritual ties to the parent," Keats adds. "They can conjure up the parent's presence when they need Mom or Dad with them."

Tina was able to use these suggestions as she worked through her mother's death and the grief that followed for many months.

"When we knew Mom was not going to live, we decided to take care of her at home. One thing we always did for the holidays was bake. Every year we'd bake cookies, make gingerbread houses, and fruit cakes for my father. These were not real easy to make. The last Christmas we had with Mom, we asked her to teach us all the recipes and guide us through all the steps so that we would always know how to make everything. Mom loved the baking smells and even though she didn't say so, I knew she was glad that we got to do that.

"Now three years later, my older sisters all come home for Christmas and we bake. Dad learned how to make his own fruitcakes, and he says Mom would be proud of him. We talk about Mom and as the smells fill the whole house, it's as if she's there with us, kind of like her spirit is there."

Keats encourages teens to dream about the parent so that they can feel close to their mother or father again. Giving suggestions to your subconscious that you'd like to visit with your parent may open up your dream experiences. A dream can transcend the feelings of loss so that the teen might feel that he hasn't lost that parent totally.

"I had a really neat dream about my dad about eight months after he was killed in a car accident," Ty said. "I was at a beach, which was a place he loved to take us. I was walking along the shore, and up ahead I could see my dad. I called to him, and he turned and waved. I couldn't catch up to him, but I wasn't really trying to either. It was like I knew I couldn't get close enough to touch him, but at least I could see him and wave. It gave me a kind of peaceful feeling. I wasn't frustrated or angry in the dream.

"When I woke up in the morning, I wrote the dream down so I would remember it. I described what Dad was wearing and how he looked. I think that was a turning point for me. I had been very angry before that, mad at him for dying and leaving us. I started to lose some of that and took a few steps toward accepting that he was gone for good but that my life is going on without him. I had wanted to stop time, sort of freeze myself so I didn't have to go on, and that wasn't working. The dream helped me start to put it behind me."

There are different types of counseling. You may feel more comfortable one-on-one with a therapist who tunes in to your feelings, moves you through resolving the confusion and grief and working toward acceptance.

"My mom took me to her counselor after my stepfather died of a heart attack right in front of all of us," Mary said. "Dad had raised me since I was three years old and was more of a father to me than my real father was. I had been having nightmares and couldn't sleep at all. I was a real mess. The funny thing was I didn't think I needed help. I was fine. No big deal. Then as I went to Linda for a few sessions I could look at myself in the mirror and see the bags under my eyes and the fear in my eyes and that's when I knew I couldn't deal with his dying all alone. I needed someone."

Having someone who is professionally trained to guide you through the grieving process can bring you to a resolution of your grief in a healthier way than if you keep on trying to handle it alone.

Counselors are trained to work in different ways. One counselor may have you sit and talk about your parent, letting out your feelings and emotions. The therapist can help you explore and let go of the stuff you might be keeping locked away inside you. By moving through the pain, experiencing it in the safety of a trained counselor's presence, you can walk on your path to recovery in a healthy way.

Another counselor may have you do imaging. Perhaps through music you will "journey" through your consciousness in an imagery where you will say good-bye to your deceased parent and cut the ties that may be keeping you stuck in your grief.

Finishing your grief and saying good-bye to your beloved parent is to recover fully. This idea of finishing comes from a therapy called Gestalt therapy. The goal is to experience all your grief feelings and let them go to allow you to renew life and live again with a new perspective.

Perhaps the counselor may have you write a letter to your mother or father who died. You may need to pour out all those feelings still left and say good-bye. Another counselor may have you sit opposite an empty chair and tell your parent all the final things you need to tell him or her. Or perhaps the counselor will "be" your parent and have you say the things you need to say and have you say what your parent would respond with. This way you could have a final conversation. This helps complete the process. Many people say, "If only I could talk to her one more time." This is the opportunity.

How the counselor helps you to deal with your grief and finish the process is up to you and the counselor. Some people choose to do a short-term counseling program, maybe six to ten sessions. Others may feel the need for a longer time. Facing and working through the crisis of your parent's death can be eased by working with someone trained to help the process.

CHAPTER 15

Acceptance, Recovery, Growth

Despite the most painful times in your mourning, you *can* recover from your grief. You should be able at some point to start feeling again that you can live a full life. As hard as it may be to believe this, you can enjoy living without feeling angry or guilty or overcome with pain.

If you have successfully resolved your grief, you will reach the place where you can accept the death of your parent in your mind and in your heart. When you feel ready to get on with your life knowing you'll be okay— that you can make it without your parent—then you are recovering.

All the intense feelings that you've experienced for what seems like such a long time lose the powerful effect they had and disappear. The wound is still there in your heart, but it's smoothing over now, and it's not so noticeable. You don't have to touch the hurt constantly to make sure it is real and not imagined. The scar tissue leaves a bump in your life, but you can rub the wound and it doesn't hurt as severely as it once did.

You won't forget about your mother or your father, but the anguish and the terrible pain associated with your loss lessens. Your reactions to the death and separation you've experienced will not be so intense.

Once you begin to live your life each day as it unfolds, you are in recovery. You'll find that you are able to get back into a comfortable routine of living without your parent's everyday presence. Hope returns to your heart and you will find that you've been through the darkest night and have made it to the dawn.

Tara said, "I guess I *knew* that I had gotten through the worst when I could turn around and say that I couldn't wait for it to be summer or Christmas or something like that. I *knew* that Mom would not be there and it was okay. I could enjoy times without her."

Whether you are aware of it or not, you most likely have special strengths that are helping you face the death of your parent. One of these is a support system. All the people who are in your life can form a network of support. Remember all those people at the funeral who said they wanted to help you in any way they could? "Call me if you need anything," they told you.

Shift away from your isolation and reach out. Call your aunt who said she would take you shopping any time you wanted. When you are stuck for a ride somewhere, ask the person down the street who offered help. Seek out the teacher who told you his father had died also when he was in his teens—he really knows what you are going through and can listen and share some insights.

Activities can also be a source of your network of support. Getting out and pitching in at the car wash that your church is holding to raise money for a family whose house burned down will lift your spirits. Diverting your energy from grief to helpfulness transforms that energy and gives you back some good feelings. Play on the softball team or help coach your little brother's basketball team. This will create feelings of satisfaction in your life, again helping you create positive experiences to replace the sadness. The more good feelings you pour into your heart, the less room there will be for pain.

Understanding and supporting yourself moves you along in recovering from grief also. Repeating special daily sayings, called affirmations, to yourself, will give your mind the opportunity to absorb positive thoughts. Affirmations such as, "Each day I feel better about myself," or "I can create my own happiness each day" give you a different outlook. It's sort of like reprogramming your internal computer that helps determine what kind of day and what sort of life you can have.

Another special strength you can be in touch with is having a purpose in life. Knowing that you are unique and have gifts to give the world will steer you back onto the road of living. Take this purpose and use it to help others. One teen whose mother had died, after she had resolved much of her own grief, helped to start a kids' grief group at the local mental health center. She volunteered her time to meet once a week with a psychologist and a group of children who had lost a parent through death. In this way of helping others, she further healed her own life.

Gaining and sharing knowledge can be another strength you can develop. As you are mourning, it might be helpful to read books about death, grief, and others' experiences. It is mentally healthy to find out as much information as you need about grief and mourning as a way of coping with the situation you are in. You can release some of your doubts about whether you can handle it, and if you'll ever make it through this time of your life, by reading others' stories of how *they* survived the death of loved ones. You'll find comfort in knowing you are not alone in this, and you're not, and you'll create hope for yourself by realizing that it is possible to live life after mom or dad is gone.

In the years you've lived your life, you know that it has its ups and downs. Life's twists and turns keep you on your toes, insisting that you learn how to adapt mentally, emotionally, physically, and spiritually. All these demands you encounter in life are really opportunities to cope and to grow. Now you probably aren't saying. "Thank you, life, for this wonderful opportunity," but if you can change your perspective a bit to say, "All right, I've been through the worst and I'm making it. I am stronger because of this," then you are maturing. If you can look at this time in your life as a big step in growing stronger and maturing in your outlook to meet life's challenges, then you've taken advantage of the opportunity.

If you have never thought of yourself as courageous, then look again. Learning to have courage to face tragedy is never an easy process. Courage is learned many times through scary processes. You may think, I can never do this. Then something, somewhere in the back of your mind or in the depth of your heart, answers back, yes, I can.

You might feel you have no choice. One young man whose grandfather died soon after his father, found that there was no other path to take.

"People would say to me, 'I don't know how you are getting through this. How can you cope?'" he said. "What else could I do? Was there another way? I don't think so. This was it. You just do it."

As you go through your grief experience you will find that honesty helps. Even the youngest children can be helped to deal with death if it is approached honestly. No lies, no deceit. Just truth and support. That's what is necessary to cope effectively with your loss.

As you go through your grieving process, you will look at what's important in life, what really counts. You will do a lot of thinking about your values in life, what's important in living, and your ideas about your life's purpose. Death is also part of life. It is inevitable for all of us, and experiencing it early in life gives you the opportunity to grow and mature. You can turn it around for yourself and then help others deal with the low blows that knock everyone off their feet. You eventually learn and know, really know, that you *can* get back on your feet and move forward, and that makes your life richer.

When you meet death, it may remind you of your own mortality. Some of you might start worrying about your own death. This thought process may give you a better look at how *you* want to live your life. Can you give it more meaning? Can you open yourself up to limitless possibilities? You've made it through a very, very stressful and painful time. Can you turn it around now and see your own growth? Do you look at life a little differently and resolve to make yours special and more purposeful?

Even if you don't see it now, you will later on. As adults, if you have grieved successfully and resolved your grief, you will look back on this time as one of incredible growth and realize that you found the strength and courage to live life to the fullest as never before.

As you encounter and accept the death and loss of your parent, you will probably question your own belief system. What used to be important may not seem so anymore. You might realize that there are other things that are more important now. You may begin to cherish other family members more because of all that you have gone through together, and life and death change things dramatically.

You may also understand love differently. Love doesn't die when your parent dies. You will realize that loving others doesn't block out the love you have for your mother or father who died. It just expands your capacity for giving and loving. Being successful at resolving grief frees you up to change, grow, and experience life as you never had before.

You are different, no doubt about that. Going through what you have experienced will change you, your outlook, your acceptance of others and events in your life. You will mature and become more resilient. You will be better able to choose what's important.

The death of your father or mother is so painful that in most cases it is *the* turning point in your life. It may not seem that way at first. Few people can be in the beginning stages of grief and say, "Oh yes, this is an incredible growth time for me and I welcome it." But in retrospect, as you travel the path that you are now on, you will look at life differently.

You are launched into a new life. All the changes that this death brings, internal and external, alter your life completely. But the grief experience can be meaningless if you don't learn how to use it. Grief can be the path to immense personal growth, and the possibilities that can grow from it are limitless.

The strength you cultivate within yourself as you resolve and accept your loss will serve you time and time again when life's hard knocks resound at your door. As you meet disappointment, sadness, or tragedy in the future, you have an inner resource now—courage to face it and move through the hard time. You've done it already. You can do it again. You can be a creative survivor. You can use this experience to reach out and embrace life to the fullest. Life is short and there's so much you can do and so many people you can touch by sharing the inner strength you've developed during this time.

As a survivor, it is normal to ask, Why me? Why do I have to go through this? It is also normal, after walking the long road of grief, to emerge with a new resolve—to make your life better. It may be to honor your mother or father, or to live your life in the way they would have wanted. It might come from knowing that you've been chosen to grow, and you can share that with others and help them develop their strengths in a time of despair.

Many people use their experiences with death and grief to go on to help others through counseling and healing work. A teenager whose brother was killed by a drunk driver speaks out at high school assemblies as a member of SADD (Students Against Driving Drunk). People work for safer highways, gun control, cancer research, and AIDS interventions all as results of experiencing the death of a loved one.

Elisabeth Kübler-Ross, who has worked with death, dying, and grief much of her life, says that many people face all the hardships of life, all the trials and tests and nightmares and losses as punishments or negative things. She feels that nothing that comes to you is negative. All the losses you experience and that you think you never can make it through, are gifts—opportunities to grow.

Dr. Kübler-Ross has lived her beliefs. She has taken what she has learned of death and grief, and the strength that can evolve from this, and made it her life's work.

You can too. However you have been changed by your mother's death or the loss of your father, you too can find love and growth in the experience. You can heal and touch others on their path to healing.

Grief is the price you pay for having loved someone. You can use it to enrich your life, your existence here on earth.

You have made it through the worst pain you can imagine.

You can go on carrying the love with you.

You can heal.

You can touch others.

You are very special.

CHAPTER 16

Keeping Memories Alive

"**A**fter my father died," Lou, thirteen, said, "I kept having this memory. I remember once when Dad was mowing the lawn. We had this big ride-on mower and he was whipping around the yard really fast. Well, he mowed too close to the clothes line and hooked some of the clothes hanging there and pulled the whole line down. It was dragging after him, pole, line, and clean laundry, and he didn't even know it! We had to run after him screaming to stop. We pointed at the mess dragging behind him and he turned around. I'll never forget the look on his face! We laughed for a week about that.

"A few days after the funeral, I thought about what we called the clothes mower day and I couldn't stop laughing. I think my brother thought I was crazy, but when I reminded him about it he started laughing like crazy too. We laughed so hard, we cried, and it helped. Then we'd tell someone else and laugh again. It's good to have a funny memory about Dad. I don't want it all to just be sad."

For however many years you spent with your parent before he or she died, you built memories. Some are funny. Others are special. Remember when the whole family went canoeing and you tipped over? Your mom said she didn't know how heavy shoes were until they got wet. So she kicked them off and then could only find one shoe. She had to go home without it.

Or how about the time when your family was chosen to light the church candles at the Christmas Eve service in front of everyone. You were nervous, but holding your father's hand as you walked up made you feel not so scared. His smiling face told you how proud he was of his family and how much he loved all of you.

Now you wish you could live some of these memories over again. With Mom or Dad gone, there won't be any more opportunities to build memories with them. That hurts. So what can you do to help ease that pain, that emptiness over the months, over the years?

"One thing that my mother did after Dad died of cancer," Nancy, fifteen, said, "was make each of us kids a Daddy & Me book. She put together pictures from when I was born up until a few weeks before he died. I have this nice photo album now that I can take out and look at whenever I want, or need to.

"There's pictures of Daddy holding me in the hospital right after I was born. Every birthday party picture has Dad doing something crazy with me and my friends, like roller skating with us, or taking us all to the beach. There's a great one of him pitching to me in a Dad and Daughter softball game that I really like to look at and remember, because I play softball on my high school team now, and I can remember all he taught me about playing.

"I think the one I love the most was one of the last ones I have of him and me at my eighth grade graduation. He was just home from his operation in the hospital, but he came to my graduation. Said he wouldn't miss it for the world. We took lots of pictures that night. I think we did because we sort of knew he might not be around for any other graduation. That's the last one in my book because he died a few months later.

"Sometimes I put the book away for a while and almost forget about it. But there's always something that reminds me, and I look at it once in a while. I like to think it's Dad sending me a message not to forget him. The book helps. I do get sad though, because all the pictures stop when I was thirteen, and there won't ever be any more pictures of my father and me. When I graduate from high school and college, he won't be there. When I get married he won't be in any of the pictures. That hurts when I think about it. I miss him a lot."

Keeping memories alive in your heart and mind will help in your healing. There's all kinds of memories— lessons about life that your parents taught you, sports they helped you learn, books they read to you. It's a special way to keep a little of your mother or father with you as you let go of pain and sadness because they are not there in your life physically anymore.

"I never told anyone about this, but about a year after Mom died I was walking in the mall," Jamie, seventeen, said. "As this lady went by, I smelt that she was wearing my mother's perfume. I closed my eyes for a minute and just stood there and smelled my mother again. It was such a nice feeling, and I got a little teary. My girlfriend wanted to know what was wrong, but I told her nothing much, just that I was remembering my mother and all the times she'd taken us to this mall.

"Then my friend and I started talking about how we wouldn't let my mother walk with us one time because there were some boys we knew there and we didn't want to be seen with a parent. She was really cool about it. She also used to buy us pizza in one pizza place when we were done shopping, and we'd show each other all the things we had bought. All these memories came back just from smelling that lady's perfume.

"When I went home that night, I went into my father's room. He still hadn't gotten rid of everything yet, and I found her perfume. I put on a little bit of her perfume at night sometimes when I missed her, so that I could smell her again. I never told anyone that I did this, I thought they'd think I was weird or something. But I don't care. It helps me remember my mother and I think that's okay."

One family's father died a few months before their yearly ski trip. Each Christmas vacation, they'd go to this one ski place for a week, and it was the only time their father would wear this cowboy hat they had given him one Christmas. He said it was the only place he felt like wearing it. It reminded him of Christmas, and Christmas was always linked with skiing.

The first year the family went skiing without their father, they took along his cowboy hat anyway. They said if they couldn't have him around, at least they'd have his hat to remind them of better times.

Memories can be of quiet times, funny, crazy times, or just feeling the feelings you had when you and your parent would do something together. No human being is perfect, so be careful about making all your memories of your parent into perfection. It's okay to remember how your mom would bug you about keeping your room clean, or how your dad had to remind you to feed the cats. Everyday memories work also to keep your parent in your life, even if it is in a different way. You don't have to be totally cut off from them. You can keep little memories around you for comfort.

"On Sunday afternoons, Dad and I would walk our Irish setter down to the lake," Trevor, twelve, said. "After he died, I walked Red alone on Sundays, but I didn't like it at first. I tried to do it like Dad by bringing other people along, like my little brother or my mother. It wasn't the same. The I tried my uncle, and the guy Mom started to go out with. It still didn't seem right, so I stopped doing it.

"But you know what happened? Red would bother me all Sunday afternoon, and Mom would say, take him for a walk. He bothered me so much that I finally took him to the lake again. There was this older guy there that day with his dog, and we got to talking. His wife had just died and he was really lonely, so I told him about my father, and we walked together. We made a deal to walk our dogs there on Sundays so we wouldn't feel so lonely. It's not my father, but it's the closest I've found, and it helps. Sometimes I pretend that it is Dad walking there with me. I think I'll keep doing this for a while because it reminds me of my father, and I don't want to forget."

Jill had an experience a few months after her mother died.

"I went blank one day and couldn't remember what my mother looked like. It scared me so much. I mean, how could I forget? So my father found a picture of Mother and himself hugging at someone's party, and had big copies made of it. We got them all framed, and put one in each of our rooms, and in the living room. My older brother put his away. He said he didn't want to be reminded for now, but I think he takes it out when he's alone in his room. It's good to have Mother's pictures around. I can remember her smiling and happy, instead of how sick she was before she died."

Keeping an article of clothing, a favorite blanket, wearing a special piece of your mother's jewelry—all these can help you keep a connection with your parent who died. Smelling his after-shave, playing her favorite song, sitting in his chair wrapped up in his flannel shirt can help you keep a bit of the closeness you felt that you cannot physically feel anymore.

"My dad used to put on coffee every morning when he got up for work. He didn't drink it, only my mother did," Tamara, eighteen, said. "After she was killed by a drunk driver, I told him not to make it anymore, that it was stupid and I didn't want to smell her coffee in the mornings. So he stopped. I guess he thought he was helping me, but I was so upset that I actually didn't know what I wanted.

"One morning I got up before him. The house was so quiet and empty and I wanted my mother back to fill up the emptiness. So I put on her coffee. When that coffee smell filled the house things felt almost right again, if you can understand that. That morning I drank the coffee, her coffee, and I felt closer to her. Now my father gets up and makes me the coffee, although we really know he's still making it for my mother."

Keeping up with rituals and ceremonies that you used to do with your parent can help you ease the pain. Even though there is a part that's missing, you can feel some comfort in keeping tradition going. At a point you will adjust to a newer, revised ritual, and then that will start feeling normal. That will tell you that you are in the healing stages, and that you are accepting your loss and moving on with your life.

It doesn't always come easily or quickly. Trevor tried to

substitute other people for his father when he walked their dog. After giving it a try, he gave it up. But it had a strong pull for him to keep on doing it, so he tried again. This time he was able to adjust to a different ritual—an older man who was just as lonely as he was. Trevor found a way to help someone else while helping himself at the same time.

The same was true for Tamara and the coffee. She stopped the smell of coffee in the mornings for a while, but it became too much of an emptiness. She was able to turn it around for herself and her father so that they could both get comfort in the morning routine.

Memories have an important place in your grieving process. If you shut out all the memories because you want to shut out the pain, you won't be helping yourself. It will take you that much longer to deal finally with your grief and to move along on the road to recovery. Laughing, crying, and remembering special moments and times you spent with your parent who died brings comfort and a release of the pain. At some point you must face your parent's death and come to terms with the loss in your life. Memories can help ease that path a bit. Remember with love.

CHAPTER ◇ 17

My Story

My own journey through grief began in 1989. My husband, Hank Grosshandler, was dying of cancer. I thought that I was so well prepared. Being a counselor, I had already read books about dealing with death and the emotions that come with it, and I thought that I had the advantage of knowing what to expect. I thought I knew all about what I might go through if he did not recover. I thought I could face it. I was strong. It wouldn't be as bad for me as it seemed to be for other people.

I was wrong.

Hank died on April 28, 1989. I was a thirty-seven-year-old widow with three young sons, Nate, eleven, Jeff, nine, and Mike, six. I was devastated.

The chaos of emotions I experienced during the months after my husband's death left me numb, although I functioned. I did my job as a high school counselor well enough given the circumstances. I kept the house going. I took care of my children. I worked with their grief as it came up as best I could and found that I wasn't prepared to deal with all three of them and their ups and downs.

I would tell those close to me, "I wish I could tem-porarily 'freeze' the kids so I could deal with my pain," but instead I froze myself because I couldn't deal with it all.

We got through that first Father's Day, Hank's birthday, our wedding anniversary. I took the boys to Florida that summer, to Disney World and to visit relatives. My mother came with us to fill the void, that empty seat, and it helped. But I was trying too hard. I was trying to make life, as much as possible, the same as it was before Hank died.

We all went back to school without him. (He was a teacher in my high school.) The kids would come home from school in tears, sometimes with sadness and pain, blaming it on everything else because the real reason was too painful. We trudged on along this path of grief.

We went back to our Christmas week ski condo and did the holidays and vacation as we always had. No one was really happy. I kept trying to make it the same, but it wasn't.

One night in early January 1990, I fell apart. I was finally letting myself feel, and it was overwhelming. No one could take my anguish away. I thought I was going crazy. It was time to look for help. Thus began my journey though counseling, admitting my pain and facing my feelings of helplessness and hopelessness.

I was so blessed to have a close, loving family who loved me through my crazy times, who listened to my denials and my statements that "I'm fine," and who sur-rounded me with a cushion of support and help. The people I worked with in school, my guidance department, helped keep me on track, shored me up when I was disintegrating, and loved me. I couldn't see all this at the time. I could only get through each day, one at a time.

That seems to be the credo for surviving tragedies—one day at a time.

Counseling helped me survive. I could make it until the next session and then pour out my fears, my complaints, my insecurities, my anger, and despair. A few months later I felt well enough emotionally to try it on my own again.

Just when things seemed to get right-side-up again, I got sick with Lyme disease. It stressed my body and my soul, but it took the focus off the grief and centered it on me. I worried about getting well, how could I handle things if I got too sick to work, why me, why now?

My kids freaked out too. "Is Mommy going to die too?" they asked their grandmother.

I heard one of them on the phone with a friend, "Mom hasn't gotten out of bed for five days. Isn't that unusual? Don't you think it's weird? What's wrong with her?" His voice was fraught with fear.

Medication helped me feel better. Things got back on track, although most times I felt as if the "track" was careening down the side of a mountain taking us someplace we didn't want to go.

Then Mike got sick with Lyme disease too. He went into the hospital for a spinal tap and three days of intravenous treatment. By coincidence, his room was in the same hospital and down the hall from the room where I was with his dad when he died. We walked through the halls each day, Mike and I. One day I got up the courage to walk past the room where I held Hank's hand as he left this world. A mixture of feelings swarmed over me, but I kept it together. Mike came home from the hospital and spent the next month on intravenous medication, which I administered twice a day.

My Lyme disease got worse—the stress I guess—and as

soon as Mike went off the intravenous medication, I went on for a month. We made it through somehow—family and love kept us going. Emotionally, I thought I had it together until I fell apart again. I returned to counseling, using different counselors to help me put the pieces back together again. There were nights when I lost control—I screamed and cried in my room, pounding the pillows and the bed at the unfairness of life.

The boys struggled through their own grief. Sometimes they let it out and sometimes they kept it in. They had friends to talk to, wonderful uncles and aunts, and of course, Nana, to help face the loss, the void in their lives.

The milestones would come and go—basketball, baseball, and soccer games where Dad no longer coached them or encouraged them from the sidelines, promotions and graduations with only one parent in the audience, and countless other special and ordinary events in their lives without Dad.

A ceremony was held in the high school gym and a plaque was placed there for their father. It says:

Henry Grosshandler
1943–1989
Teacher, Coach, Friend

Every time we go there, or when the kids play there, we are reminded and comforted knowing that this man was respected and well-liked. It is also a reminder of what is missing from our lives.

There's one thing for sure about having someone you love die—there's no going back. We can't undo what's happened no matter how much we wish we could. We can only go on. And *how* we go on depends on each of us.

As we live through the time of mourning, days, months, years, we take little steps in working through our grief. We can't see the growth by leaps or bounds. All we can do is look back over where we've been and see the changes, the growth, the journey.

Accepting that many things are a part of normal grieving is so helpful. At the times when I felt I was losing my mind, I wish someone had said, "It's okay. This is normal. It's healing." Actually people probably did say it—I just couldn't comprehend it at the time. It takes all those little baby steps toward resolving grief and accepting the death and the feelings of loss of our loved one, to complete our journey. With the help of family, friends, counselors, and even strangers, I found my way along the path of grief.

Looking back now, years later, I can put it in a more understandable perspective. I experienced the denial, the pain, the anger, the loss, the tears, the feelings of insanity, and the depression, my "black pit" into which I would backslide, or so I felt. Actually, each time I encountered my "black pit" it was really another stop on my way through the grief. As I said before, there's no way around the pain—only through it.

So every step was perfect. It was all a tapestry of feelings and experiences that moved me through an intense time of my life, a time of growth. It's not what I had imagined my life to be. I had no choice except to deal with it as it unfolded, without a game plan, without warning of what was coming up next.

My journey through grief and loss has helped me to be a better counselor, a better Mom, a better human being. I seem to attract to me people who have suffered loss, and I feel better equipped to understand their hurt, their despair. I still cry sometimes, as the wound is not totally healed over. There will always be a void, an emptiness when I think of what could have been. But that is not to be. My life and my children's lives have taken a turn in a different direction and we go on.

I remember surprising myself about three years after Hank died. I was speaking to a friend about where I was in my life at that moment. I could honestly say that it had been an incredible few years and I wouldn't have had it any other way.

Then I stopped myself and said, "Did I actually say that?"

I never would have chosen this path, but this was what I was presented with in my life. I can see now that we are always a sum-total of our experiences. I have experienced being at someone's side as he died, been all through the whirling vortex of grief, witnessed my sons' journey through their sadness and pain, and I have recovered. I've made it through. And so can you. We all have that inner strength to do this—all in our own time and way.

My son, Nate, now sixteen, says that the hardest parts were the sadness and the feelings of being alone after his dad died. Sometimes strong feelings come up even now, five years later. Nate still misses him around the house; he misses doing things together like participating in sports as they always had.

"I remember Dad would get mad at me sometimes when I'd fool around," Nate said. "So now I think about him if I'm not giving my best, you know? I'll say to myself, 'What am I doing? What is Dad thinking now, seeing me fool around? What would he think of me?' Then I'll turn it around and work harder and try to do better, for him."

What is Nate's advice for getting through the sadness and the pain?

"Keep on doing the things that make you happy, like participating in a sport. Don't stop doing what you like just because of what you lost. Keep on going."

Mike was six when his dad died. Now he's eleven. He remembers that after Hank died he had no one to throw him up high in the pool like his dad did. Now Mike has to play baseball with his mom or his friends instead of his dad.

Mike says, "Try to fill that spot with all the activities you used to do with your parent who died. Try to fill it up with your other parent, or friends or brothers or sisters."

This is advice from two young people who have been where you are now. Keep on living. Stay with your activities, stay involved in the fun things you've always done. Life goes on.

No two experiences of grief are the same. Yours are unique as mine were, as my sons' were. However, there will be similarities. I hope this book will help you realize that you are doing a fine job in dealing with your grief, and I admire you for your strength and courage. You are a survivor.

You are resilient and have a great capacity to cope with problems. As each spring season begins anew, so shall you. No matter how much we suffer, we will grow. So feel that little seed of hope sprouting inside your heart. Get in touch with the courage within you to travel your journey through the pain. It's the only way to make it. And you *will* make it.

Help List

What you can do to help yourself grieve:

Read books, pamphlets, magazine articles, about death and grieving. There is an index of books at the end.

Go to your local library. There are books about death for all age groups, and most situations.

Write for copies of *Bereavement: A Magazine of Hope and Healing*, Bereavement Publishing, 8133 Telegraph Drive, Colorado Springs, CO 80902.

Every funeral home has pamphlets about grief. They will mail you some if you ask, or if you can't, ask a friend to call.

Support groups are everywhere. Call any hospital and ask for their community services for bereavement. There are groups for children and pre-teens (Art Therapy Workshops), for teens, for parents, spouses, etc.

Local Hospice programs, run by hospitals or local organizations, help families with a loved one who is terminally ill. They stay in close touch with you after the death and help you find a way to deal with your grief.

There are lectures and workshops in your town or county. You can call your county social services office or your town or city's municipal offices for information.

Every funeral home has information and usually has certified bereavement counselors working for it. These counselors can provide you with things you can read and do for your grief. They also may run group sessions for six to ten weeks for people or teens just like you.

Your church, synagogue, mosque, or temple can provide you with counseling and information about grief support groups or lectures.

Private counselors or therapists who are experienced in grief counseling are also available. You can get information from the yellow pages of the phone book, or through your school counselor, or through any of the organizations mentioned above.

There is much help out there if you choose to seek it. You will find that in sharing with others, your grief will be made a little easier in the long run.

Glossary

affirmation   A positive saying used to make changes in life.

AIDS   Syndrome in which your immune system is unable to fight off diseases.

alcoholism   An illness in which there is a strong desire to continue drinking alcoholic beverages.

bereavement   The state of being sad and lonely because someone has been taken away from you, usually by death.

counseling   Talking together with another who can help or advise you on how to deal with a situation.

cremation   The burning of a dead body to ashes.

denial   Refusing to recognize or accept.

depression   Overwhelming sadness and gloominess.

executor   A person who has been named to carry out the terms of another person's will.

foster care   When a child who has no family to care for him/her has a home and family chosen for him/her.

Gestalt therapy   A type of counseling in which people work on their patterns of experiences.

grief   Deep and painful sorrow, as that which is caused by a loved one's death.

guardian   A person chosen by parents or the courts to take charge of a child.

HIV   The human immunodeficiency virus which attacks the body's immune system; it is believed to cause the disease known as AIDS.

immortality   Living forever, never dying.

inheritance   That which you receive from someone when they die.

insurance   A contract by which a company agrees to pay a person an amount of money in case of loss by fire, theft, death.

mourning   The act of showing sadness or sorrow over someone's death.

near-death experience   A happening claimed by many who have been close to death or have actually "died" and been revived.

overdose   To take too large an amount of a drug.

psychic   A person who has special mental and spiritual abilities who may seem to read your mind.

psychotherapist   A person trained in counseling and treatment of depression and mental illnesses.

recovery   A return to good health or normal circumstances.

reincarnation   The belief that souls live different lifetimes in different bodies.

resentment   A feeling of bitter hurt and anger.

Social Security   A system of government insurance for making payments to those who are retired, unable to work, or are the minor child of someone who died but paid into the system.

suicide   The taking of one's own life; killing oneself.

trustee   A person who is put in charge of the property, money, or affairs of another person.

trust fund   Money set aside and kept for another.

For Further Reading

ARTICLES

Beach, Mari Hardiman, "The Spirit of Elisabeth Kübler-Ross," *Venture Inward*, Nov./Dec. 1990.

Gilbert, Sara D., "Learning to Live with a Single Parent," *Careers*, Sept./Oct. 1990.

Lightner, Candy, and Hathaway, Nancy. "The Other Side of Sorrow," *Ladies' Home Journal*, September 1990.

BOOKS

Bradley, Buff. *Endings: A Book about Death.* Reading, MA: Addison-Wesley Publishing Co., 1979.

Cayce, Hugh Lynn. *God's Other Door.* Virginia Beach, VA: A.R.E. Press, 1987.

Colgrove, Melba, Ph.D., Harold H. Bloomfield, M.D., and Peter A. McWilliams. *How to Survive the Loss of a Love.* New York: Bantam Books, 1976.

Grollman, Earl A. *Straight Talk About Death for Teenagers,* Boston, MA.: Beacon Press, 1993.

Heegaard, Marge Eaton. *Death and Grief.* Minneapolis: Lerner Publishing Company, 1990.

James, John K., and Frank Cherry. *The Grief Recovery Handbook.* New York: Harper & Row, Publishers, 1988.

Krementz, Jill. *How It Feels When a Parent Dies.* New York: Alfred Knopf, 1981.

Kübler-Ross, Elisabeth. *On Children and Death.* New York: Macmillan Publishing Company, 1983.

——————*On Death and Dying.* New York: Macmillan Publishing Company, 1969.

Leshan, Eda. *Learning to Say Good-By.* New York: Avon Books, 1976.

Raab, Robert, A. *Coping with Death*, rev. ed. New York: The Rosen Publishing Group, 1989.

Rando, Theresa A. *Grief, Dying, and Death.* Champaign, IL: Research Press Company, 1984.

Richter, Elizabeth. *Losing Someone You Love.* New York: G.P. Putnam's Sons, 1986.

Rodegast, Pat, and Judith Stanton. *Emmanuel's Book.* New York: Bantam Books, 1987.

Rofes, Eric E. and The Unit at Fayerweather Street School. *The Kids' Book about Death and Dying.* Boston, MA: Little, Brown, and Company, 1985.

Siegel, Bernie, M.D. *Love, Medicine, & Miracles.* New York: Harper & Row, Publishers, 1986.

Staudacher, Carol. *Beyond Grief—A Guide for Recovering from the Death of a Loved One.* Oakland, CA: New Harbinger Press, 1987.

Strauss, Linda L. *Coping When a Parent Has Cancer.* New York: The Rosen Publishing Group, 1988.

Tatelbaum, Judy. *The Courage to Grieve.* New York: Harper & Row, Publishers, 1980.

Viorst, Judith. *Necessary Losses.* New York: Simon and Schuster, 1986.

Index